GUIDE TO FOOD STORAGE

Follow this guide for food storage, and you can be sure that what's in your freezer, refrigerator, and pantry is fresh-tasting and ready to use in recipes.

IN THE FREEZER
(At -10° to 0° F)

DAIRY

Cheese, hard	3 months
Cheese, soft	2 weeks
Egg substitute	6 months
Egg whites	6 months
Egg yolks	8 months
Ice cream, sherbet	1 month

FRUITS AND VEGETABLES

Commercially frozen fruits	1 year
Commercially frozen vegetables	8 to 12 months

MEATS, POULTRY, AND SEAFOOD
Beef, Lamb, and Veal

Ground, uncooked, and all cuts, cooked	3 months
Roasts and steaks, uncooked	9 months

Pork

Ground, uncooked, and all cuts, cooked	3 months
Roasts and chops, uncooked	6 months

Poultry

All cuts, cooked	1 month
Boneless or bone-in pieces, uncooked	6 months

Seafood

Bass, perch, trout, and shellfish	3 months
Cod, flounder, and halibut	6 months

IN THE REFRIGERATOR
(At 34° to 40° F)

DAIRY

Butter	4 months
Buttermilk	1 to 2 weeks
Cheese, block	3 to 4 weeks
Cheese, commercial grated Parmesan	1 year
Cream cheese, fat-free, light, and ⅓-less-fat	2 weeks
Egg substitute, opened	3 days
Fresh eggs in shell	1 month

MEATS, POULTRY, AND SEAFOOD
Beef, Lamb, Pork, and Veal

Ground and stew meat, uncooked	1 to 2 days
Roasts, uncooked	2 to 4 days
Steaks and chops, uncooked	3 to 5 days

Chicken, Turkey, and Seafood

All cuts, uncooked	1 to 2 days

FRUITS AND VEGETABLES

Apples, beets, cabbage, carrots, celery, citrus fruits, eggplant, and parsnips	2 to 3 weeks
Apricots, asparagus, berries, cauliflower, cucumbers, mushrooms, okra, peaches, pears, peas, peppers, plums, salad greens, and summer squash	2 to 4 days
Corn, husked	1 day

IN THE PANTRY
Keep these at room temperature for 6 to 12 months.

BAKING AND COOKING STAPLES
Baking powder
Biscuit and baking mix
Broth, canned
Cooking spray
Honey
Mayonnaise, fat-free, low-fat, and light (unopened)
Milk, canned evaporated fat-free
Milk, nonfat dry powder
Mustard, prepared (unopened)
Oils, olive and vegetable
Pasta, dried
Peanut butter
Rice, instant and regular
Salad dressings, bottled (unopened)
Seasoning sauces, bottled
Tuna, canned

FRUITS, LEGUMES, AND VEGETABLES
Fruits, canned
Legumes (beans, lentils, peas), dried or canned
Tomato products, canned
Vegetables, canned

Tiramisù, page 52

Gnocchi with Pumpkin and
Sage, page 90

Barley Salad with Asparagus
and Arugula, page 167

Pesto Lasagna with Bolognese and Garlic Cream, page 123

WeightWatchers®

Quick Italian
Favorites

Oxmoor
House®

©2006 by Oxmoor House, Inc.

Book Division of Southern Progress Corporation

P.O. Box 2262, Birmingham, Alabama 35201-2262

ISBN-13: 978-0-8487-3118-2

ISBN-10: 0-8487-3118-2

Library of Congress Control Number: 2006925271

Printed in the United States of America

First Printing 2006

Be sure to check with your health-care provider before making any changes in your diet.

WeightWatchers® and *POINTS*® are registered trademarks of *Weight Watchers* International, Inc., and are used under license by Healthy Living, Inc.

OXMOOR HOUSE, INC.

Editor in Chief: Nancy Fitzpatrick Wyatt

Executive Editor: Katherine M. Eakin

Copy Chief: Allison Long Lowery

WeightWatchers® **Quick Italian Favorites**

Foods Editor: Alyson Moreland Haynes

Assistant Editor: Terri Laschober

Copy Editor: Diane Rose

Editorial Assistants: Julie Boston; Rachel Quinlivan, R.D.

Director, Test Kitchens: Elizabeth Tyler Austin

Assistant Director, Test Kitchens: Julie Christopher

Food Stylist: Kelley Self Wilton

Test Kitchens Professionals: Kristi Carter, Nicole Lee Faber, Kathleen Royal Phillips, Elise Weis

Photography Director: Jim Bathie

Senior Photo Stylist: Kay E. Clarke

Photo Stylist: Katherine Eckert

Publishing Systems Administrator: Rick Tucker

Director of Production: Laura Lockhart

Production Manager: Greg A. Amason

Production Assistant: Faye Porter Bonner

Contributors

Designer: Nancy Johnson

Indexer: Mary Ann Laurens

Interns: Meg Kozinsky, Ashley Leath, Caroline Markunas, Vanessa Rusch Thomas

Photographers: Beau Gustafson, Lee Harrelson

COVER: Spaghetti and Meatballs, page 106

To order additional publications, call 1-800-765-6400.

For more books to enrich your life, visit oxmoorhouse.com

Contents

INTRODUCTION

RECIPES

The Healthy Italian Kitchen

Prepare great meals for family and friends with minimal effort and little time using these healthy classic Italian recipes from **WeightWatchers®**

Italian cuisine is the most popular ethnic food in America, and since it's rich in fruits, vegetables, grains, and unsaturated fats, it has an important place in a healthy diet. In this cookbook, you'll find Italian-American favorites and authentic recipes from across Italy plus good nutrition, easy-to-find ingredients, and simplified cooking procedures on every page. We think you'll enjoy preparing these recipes and learning about Italian traditions as much as you'll savor these dishes with family and friends.

The basic ingredients of Italian cooking are more common than you might think. Check out our list of Mediterranean Staples below for items to keep on hand. Read on for some truly genuine Italian ingredients that you must try.

Anchovies, which are mostly regarded as a pizza topping in America, play a flavorful role in many sauces and dressings, such as *Raw Vegetables with Warm Anchovy-Garlic Sauce,* page 18; *Turkey Tonnato,* page 98; and *Puttanesca Sauce,* page 128. For more anchovy facts, see page 18.

Fennel lends a unique licorice flavor to many Italian dishes. Try this native Mediterranean vegetable in *Chilled Fennel Soup,* page 179; *Baked Fennel with Roasted Red Peppers and Asiago*

MEDITERRANEAN STAPLES
Keep these items stocked in your pantry and fridge for cooking with Italian flair.

Olive oil
Vinegars *(aceto):*
    balsamic, red wine,
    white wine
Red wine/white wine
Coarse salt
Crushed red pepper flakes
Black peppercorns
Dried herbs: rosemary,
    thyme, basil, herbes de
    Provence
Bottled roasted red bell
    peppers

Olives (kalamata, cracked
    Sicilian green)
Canned tomatoes
Canned tuna
Anchovies
Capers
Assorted legumes:
    canned cannellini
    beans, canned chick-
    peas, dried lentils
Bottled marinara sauce
Bottled pesto
Arborio rice

Dried pasta (assorted
    shapes)
Cornmeal
Sun-dried tomatoes
Garlic
Onion: Spanish, red,
    sweet, shallots, cipollini
Potatoes
Nuts: almonds,
    walnuts, hazelnuts,
    pine nuts
Cheeses: Asiago,
    Parmesan, Romano

Cheese, page 139; and *Italian Vegetable Caponata,* page 148. Find more information on page 139.

Flavor-infused olive oils may be more expensive than regular olive oil, but they can make a dish extraspecial without any fuss. See if you don't agree when you use one in *Charred Cauliflower,* page 137; *Risi e Bisi,* page 150; or *Insalata di Frutti di Mare,* page 168. You can purchase these oils in small amounts, which offsets the cost.

Mascarpone: Relish this fresh cheese's lush texture in *Cherries in Chianti with Honeyed Mascarpone Cream,* page 36; *Warm Hazelnut Pears with Sweet Mascarpone Cream,* page 40; or *Tiramisù,* page 52. To learn more about mascarpone, see page 36.

Marzipan, made from almond paste, sugar, and sometimes egg whites, can be colored and shaped for decoration or incorporated into desserts. Look for it canned or in plastic-wrapped logs in large supermarkets. Give it a try in *Italian Almond Cake,* page 54.

Pancetta, made from the same cut of meat as bacon, is cured and rubbed with aromatic spices and/or herbs. Unlike bacon, it maintains a firm texture when simmered in liquids. Try *Brussels Sprouts with Pancetta,* page 132; *Lentil Soup with Pancetta and Parmesan,* page 184; or *Potato Chowder with Pancetta and Rosemary,* page 185.

Parmigiano-Reggiano, which is aged a minimum of two years, has a sharper flavor and a crumblier texture than domestic Parmesan. Taste the difference in *Orzo with Basil, Orange, and Pine Nuts,* page 100; *Artichoke Pesto,* page 125; and *Smashed Parmesan Potatoes,* page 143.

Prosciutto (cured salt-rubbed pork leg) has a silky texture, a distinct flavor, and a low fat content. This prime ingredient stars in *Minted Peas with Prosciutto,* page 142; *Minted Prosciutto and Melon,* page 13; and *Rosemary-Prosciutto Breadsticks,* page 187. If desired, you can substitute bacon, Canadian bacon, or high-quality deli ham.

Test-Kitchen Secrets

Ensure accurate, tasty results with these tips from our Test Kitchens.

Cooking spray should never be used near direct heat. Always remove a pan from heat before spraying it with cooking spray.

Cooking with alcohol: Wines and liqueurs are part of many Italian classics, such as *Veal Marsala,* page 84; *Zuppa Inglese,* page 50; and *Tiramisù,* page 52. We offer alcohol substitutions when possible, but some flavor will be lost.

Measuring cheese: A general rule for semifirm cheeses is that ¼ cup shredded cheese equals 1 ounce. But for hard cheeses like Parmesan, this does not hold true. Go by the cup or tablespoon amount provided when measuring hard cheeses for accurate **POINTS**® values. To keep freshly shredded Parmesan on hand for easy measuring, shred the entire block, and store it in a heavy-duty zip-top plastic bag in the refrigerator for up to six months.

Toasting Nuts: We often call for nuts to be toasted to enhance their flavor. Toast them in the oven while you prepare other ingredients by baking them at 350° for 6 to 8 minutes; or cook them in a dry skillet over medium heat 1 to 2 minutes, stirring frequently.

About Our Recipes

WeightWatchers® *Quick Italian Favorites* gives you the nutrition facts you need to make your life easier. We've provided the following useful information with every recipe:

- A number calculated through the *POINTS®* Food System (a component of the *POINTS* Weight-Loss System) from *Weight Watchers* International, Inc.
- Diabetic exchange values for those who use them as a guide for planning meals
- A complete nutrient analysis per serving

POINTS Food System

Every recipe in the book includes a number calculated using the *POINTS* Food System. Each food is given a *POINTS* value based on a formula that considers the calorie, fat, and fiber content of the food. Foods with more calories and fat receive high numbers, while fruits and vegetables receive low numbers. For more information about the *Weight Watchers* program and a meeting nearest you, call 1-800-651-6000 or visit online at www.weightwatchers.com.

Diabetic Exchanges

Exchange values are provided for people with diabetes and for those who use them for calorie-controlled diets. All foods within a certain group contain approximately the same amount of nutrients and calories, so one serving of a food from a food group can be substituted or exchanged for one serving of any other item on the list. The food groups are starch, fruit, milk, vegetable, meat, and fat. The exchange values are based on the *Exchange Lists for Meal Planning* developed by the American Diabetes Association and The American Dietetic Association.

Nutrient Analysis

Each recipe has a complete list of nutrients, including calories, fat, saturated fat, protein, carbohydrates, dietary fiber, cholesterol, iron, sodium, and calcium. This information makes it easy for you to use the recipes in any weight-loss program that you may choose to follow. Measurements are abbreviated g (grams) and mg (milligrams). Numbers are based on these assumptions:

- Unless otherwise indicated, meat, poultry, and fish refer to skinned, boned, and cooked servings.
- When we give a range for an ingredient (3 to 3½ cups flour, for instance), we calculate using the lesser amount.
- When we offer an ingredient substitution, we calculate using the first ingredient given.
- Some alcohol calories evaporate during heating; the analysis reflects that.
- Only the amount of marinade absorbed by the food is used in calculation.
- Garnishes and optional ingredients are not included in an analysis.

Nutritional values used in our calculations either come from The Food Processor, Version 7.5 (ESHA Research) or are provided by food manufacturers.

Appetizers
&
Beverages

prep: 10 minutes • **cook:** 18 minutes • **other:** 30 minutes

ROASTED ALMONDS

Grown in southern Italy, almonds are used in a variety of recipes, from desserts to savory dishes. When salted and roasted, they are served as a snack, often with a glass of wine.

POINTS value:
5

exchanges:
½ starch
1 high-fat meat
2 fat

per serving:
Calories 231
Fat 20g (saturated fat 2.5g)
Protein 7.4g
Carbohydrate 7.4g
Fiber 4.4g
Cholesterol 5mg
Iron 0.1mg
Sodium 159mg
Calcium 7mg

3 cups whole almonds
2 tablespoons minced fresh rosemary
1 tablespoon chopped fresh thyme
2 tablespoons butter, melted
¾ teaspoon salt
½ teaspoon ground red pepper

1. Preheat oven to 350°.
2. Combine all ingredients in a large bowl; stir well. Spread nuts on a jelly-roll pan. Bake at 350° for 18 to 20 minutes or until toasted, stirring twice. Cool completely in pan on a wire rack. Store in an airtight container. Yield: 12 servings (serving size: ¼ cup).

Hunger-Smashing Almonds: Almonds contain more disease-fighting vitamin E than any other nut, and more than 90% of the fat is unsaturated, which is the heart–healthy kind. In addition, a handful of nuts can really satisfy your hunger, and the high fat content keeps you fuller longer, resulting in less eating overall. Roasting almonds, as in this recipe, helps release flavor compounds that make for a richer, more nutty taste.

CHEESE-STUFFED DATES WITH CRISPY PROSCIUTTO

18 whole pitted dates
18 (1 x ¼–inch) pieces ricotta salata, Parmigiano-Reggiano, or feta cheese (about 1 ounce)
6   very thin slices prosciutto (about 3 ounces), cut lengthwise into thirds

1. Preheat oven to 450°.
2. Stuff each date with 1 piece of cheese, filling the hole left by the pit. Wrap each date with a strip of prosciutto. Place wrapped dates on a baking sheet. Bake at 450° for 13 minutes or until prosciutto is crisp and cheese just begins to ooze. Serve warm or at room temperature. Yield: 6 servings (serving size: 3 stuffed dates).

POINTS value:
2

exchanges:
1½ fruit
½ high-fat meat

per serving:
Calories 121
Fat 2.5g (saturated fat 1.2g)
Protein 5.4g
Carbohydrate 21.5g
Fiber 2g
Cholesterol 12mg
Iron 0.5mg
Sodium 306mg
Calcium 36mg

MINTED PROSCIUTTO AND MELON

A quick soak in sweet wine, honey, and mint is all the melon needs—any longer and it begins to water out and dilute the flavors.

½   cup sweet Italian sparkling white wine (such as spumante) or sparkling white grape juice
1   tablespoon minced fresh mint
1   tablespoon honey
24 (1½–inch) cubes ripe cantaloupe
6   very thin slices prosciutto (about 3 ounces), cut lengthwise into 4 strips

1. Combine first 4 ingredients in a large bowl, tossing gently to coat. Cover and chill 30 minutes.
2. Remove cantaloupe, reserving marinade. Wrap cantaloupe pieces with prosciutto; secure each with a wooden pick. Serve with marinade for dipping. Yield: 6 servings (serving size: 4 pieces cantaloupe and 4 teaspoons marinade).

POINTS value:
2

exchanges:
1 fruit
½ high-fat meat

per serving:
Calories 101
Fat 1.8g (saturated fat 0.6g)
Protein 5.3g
Carbohydrate 14.8g
Fiber 0.1g
Cholesterol 8mg
Iron 0.7mg
Sodium 276mg
Calcium 16mg

WHITE BEAN DIP

With a hint of lemon and sage, this dip is a simple appetizer for casual entertaining. It's similar to hummus but has a chunkier texture than its Greek cousin. Place a bowlful of dip on a platter, and surround it with cucumber slices and carrot and celery sticks, or use it as a spread for crostini ("little crusts").

POINTS value:
1

exchange:
½ starch

per serving:
Calories 38
Fat 0.8g (saturated fat 0.1g)
Protein 1.6g
Carbohydrate 6.3g
Fiber 0.1g
Cholesterol 0mg
Iron 0.6mg
Sodium 53mg
Calcium 53mg

2   (15.5-ounce) cans cannellini beans or other white beans, drained
¼   cup chopped fresh flat-leaf parsley
¼   cup minced red onion
2   tablespoons chopped fresh sage
2   teaspoons grated fresh lemon rind
3   tablespoons fresh lemon juice
1   tablespoon olive oil
½   teaspoon salt
½   teaspoon freshly ground black pepper
3   garlic cloves, minced

1. Place beans in a large bowl, and coarsely mash with a fork or pastry blender. Add parsley and remaining ingredients, and stir well. Serve at room temperature, or cover and chill until ready to serve. Yield: 2¾ cups (serving size: 2 tablespoons).

Bread Bases: Bread is an essential part of the Italian diet and is a great base for traditional dips and spreads, as well as more elaborate toppings. Crostini (usually plain toasted bread) and bruschetta (garlic bread that's traditionally grilled) are easy to make at home.

To make crostini: Coat ½-inch slices of Italian or French bread baguette with cooking spray, and bake at 375° for 10 minutes.

To make bruschetta: Prepare grill. Place ½-inch slices of Italian or French bread baguette on a grill rack coated with cooking spray; cook 2 minutes on each side or until lightly browned. Remove from grill. Rub one side of each bread slice with cut sides of halved garlic cloves. (For instructions to make in the oven, refer to the recipe on page 20.)

If you don't have time to make your own, check your local supermarket for commercial panetini (oven-baked Italian toast), crostini, and bruschetta.

SUN-DRIED TOMATO AND OLIVE TAPENADE

Olives, capers, and anchovies come together with tangy sun-dried tomatoes to create this flavor-packed paste. Crisp, firm Belgian endive and radicchio leaves are ideal dippers, as the bitter greens pair beautifully with the salty tapenade. This spread is also tasty slathered over bread, and it perks up grilled fish and chicken.

½ cup pitted kalamata olives
2 tablespoons capers
2 tablespoons water
1 tablespoon extravirgin olive oil
½ teaspoon freshly ground black pepper
2 oil-packed anchovy fillets, drained
1 (3-ounce) package ready-to-use julienne-cut sun-dried tomatoes, packed without oil (such as Mariani)
1 garlic clove
¼ cup fresh flat-leaf parsley

POINTS value:
2

exchanges:
1½ vegetable
1 fat

per serving:
Calories 78
Fat 4.5g (saturated fat 0.6g)
Protein 1.3g
Carbohydrate 7.5g
Fiber 1.7g
Cholesterol 1mg
Iron 0.6mg
Sodium 287mg
Calcium 10mg

1. Place first 8 ingredients in a food processor; process until smooth, stopping once to scrape down sides. Add parsley, and pulse 8 to 10 times or until minced. Serve immediately, or cover and chill until ready to serve. Yield: 8 servings (serving size: 2 tablespoons).

Ready-to-Use Sun-Dried Tomatoes: Be sure to buy ready-to-use sun-dried tomatoes packed without oil for this savory spread. Because they've undergone a special process that adds back moisture, there's no need to reconstitute them, and they don't have the fat of dried tomatoes packed in oil. Like all sun-dried tomatoes, this convenient product is high in vitamin A and is a good source of potassium.

CREAMY PESTO–CHEESE SPREAD
pictured on page 24

Traditional pesto, which was created in Genoa, is a no-cook sauce made with puréed basil, pine nuts, garlic, olive oil, and Parmesan cheese. We used a commercial pesto as a shortcut to create this layered spread. You can make this appetizer as little as one day or as much as one week in advance—the longer it refrigerates, the more flavorful it becomes. Try using sun-dried tomato pesto along with the basil pesto for a festive holiday appetizer.

POINTS value:
2

exchanges:
½ starch
½ vegetable
½ fat

per serving:
Calories 79
Fat 2.6g (saturated fat 0.8g)
Protein 3.8g
Carbohydrate 10.3g
Fiber 0.5g
Cholesterol 3mg
Iron 0.6mg
Sodium 316mg
Calcium 45mg

1   (8-ounce) block fat–free cream cheese
⅓   cup (1⅓ ounces) shredded provolone cheese
3   tablespoons light mayonnaise
½   teaspoon salt
½   teaspoon cracked black pepper
½   teaspoon bottled minced garlic
2   tablespoons commercial pesto, divided
1   tablespoon thinly sliced fresh basil leaves
36   (¼-inch-thick) slices diagonally cut Italian or French bread baguette
¾   cup bottled or homemade marinara sauce (recipe on page 126)

1. Combine first 6 ingredients in a large bowl; beat with a mixer at medium speed until smooth.
2. Line a 10-ounce custard cup, small bowl, or 1-cup glass measuring cup with plastic wrap. Spread one-third of cheese mixture into bottom of prepared cup. Top with 1 tablespoon pesto, spreading to cover cream cheese mixture. Repeat procedure with one-third cheese mixture and remaining pesto; top with remaining cheese mixture. Tap cup gently against countertop to compact the layers. Cover with plastic wrap, and chill 8 hours or overnight.
3. Uncover and invert spread onto a serving plate; remove plastic wrap. Sprinkle sliced basil over top of spread. Serve with baguette slices and marinara sauce. Yield: 18 servings (serving size: 1 tablespoon cheese spread, 2 baguette slices, and 2 teaspoons marinara sauce).

MARINATED GOAT CHEESE

Italy offers a tremendous variety of cheeses made from all types of milk, including sheep, goat, and buffalo. Goat cheese has a delightfully tangy flavor that is well complemented by the fresh herbs in this robust marinade. The cheese becomes more flavorful the longer it marinates.

⅓   cup chopped sun-dried tomatoes (about 12 tomatoes), packed without oil

¼   cup olive oil

2   tablespoons chopped fresh rosemary

1   tablespoon chopped fresh basil

2   teaspoons grated fresh lemon rind

½   teaspoon crushed red pepper

½   teaspoon freshly ground black pepper

3   garlic cloves, minced

2   (4-ounce) packages goat cheese, each cut into 8 slices

16   (¼-inch-thick) slices diagonally cut Italian or French bread baguette

1. Combine tomatoes and oil in a small bowl; let stand 10 minutes. Add rosemary and next 5 ingredients; stir well.

2. Place cheese slices in an 8-inch square baking dish; pour marinade over cheese. Cover and marinate at least 4 hours. Serve with baguette slices. Yield: 16 servings (serving size: 1 cheese slice and 1 baguette slice).

POINTS value:
2

exchanges:
½ medium-fat meat
1 fat

per serving:
Calories 86
Fat 6.2g (saturated fat 3.2g)
Protein 3.8g
Carbohydrate 4.2g
Fiber 0.4g
Cholesterol 11mg
Iron 0.6mg
Sodium 129mg
Calcium 52mg

RAW VEGETABLES WITH WARM ANCHOVY–GARLIC SAUCE

At the end of the grape harvest each year in Piedmont, winemakers feast on a meal that begins with *bagna cauda* (BAHN-YAH KOW-DAH), a "hot bath" of olive oil, butter, garlic, and anchovies served with raw vegetables. The anchovies, which are loaded with bone-building calcium and heart-healthy omega-3 fatty acids, give the dip body and a slight saltiness without lending a fishy taste.

***POINTS* value:**
3

exchanges:
½ starch
½ vegetable
2 fat

per serving:
Calories 131
Fat 9.6g (saturated fat 1.5g)
Protein 1.8g
Carbohydrate 10.7g
Fiber 2.9g
Cholesterol 2mg
Iron 0.9mg
Sodium 136mg
Calcium 45mg

6   very small red potatoes (¾ pound)
½   cup olive oil
1   teaspoon butter
¼   teaspoon kosher salt
3   canned anchovy fillets, finely chopped
1   garlic clove, minced
24   baby carrots (about 6 ounces)
6   celery stalks, trimmed and quartered
1   head Belgian endive (about ¼ pound), separated into 12 leaves
½   (1¼-pound) fennel bulb, trimmed and cut lengthwise into ¼-inch slices and separated into spears

1. Steam potatoes, covered, 10 minutes or until tender. Cut each potato lengthwise into 4 wedges.
2. While potatoes cook, heat oil and butter in top of a double boiler over medium heat 2 minutes or until butter melts. Add salt, anchovies, and garlic; cook 10 minutes or until anchovies begin to dissolve and garlic is soft and fragrant (garlic should not begin to brown or take on any color). Pour sauce into a warm serving bowl; serve warm with vegetables. Yield: 12 servings (serving size: about 2 teaspoons anchovy-garlic sauce, 2 potato wedges, 2 carrots, 2 celery sticks, 1 endive leaf, and about 1 ounce fennel spears).

Note: Traditionally, the bagna cauda is served in a bowl set over chafing fuel or a tea light so that the sauce stays warm throughout the appetizer course.

ANTIPASTO WITH SUN-DRIED TOMATO MAYONNAISE

Antipasto, eaten "before the meal," is far more than a plate of cold cuts. Rather, it's a showcase of the country's wonderful bounty together on one platter—marinated, fresh, and grilled vegetables; assorted cheeses; a variety of olives; plus a choice of fish and meats. To keep this appetizer quick and simple, we've limited the selection here to some of our favorite healthful choices.

⅓   cup fat-free mayonnaise

2   tablespoons sun-dried tomato pesto (such as Classico)

8   (½-inch-thick) slices diagonally cut Italian or French bread baguette, toasted

4   (0.7-ounce) slices part-skim mozzarella cheese (such as Sargento deli-style thin slices), halved

2   (6-ounce) cans solid white albacore tuna in water, drained and flaked

1   (12-ounce) bottle pickled vegetables (such as Bella Garden Mix Giardinera), drained

½   cup pitted kalamata olives

2   ounces shaved pesto-Parmesan oven-roasted ham (such as Boar's Head) or other lean ham

POINTS value:
4

exchanges:
1 starch
2 lean meat

per serving:
Calories 195
Fat 7.6g (saturated fat 2.2g)
Protein 16.1g
Carbohydrate 13.5g
Fiber 1.2g
Cholesterol 28mg
Iron 0.9mg
Sodium 1,143mg
Calcium 84mg

1. Combine mayonnaise and pesto in a small serving bowl; stir well. Place bowl on a large platter. Arrange bread and remaining ingredients around bowl on platter. Serve immediately. Yield: 8 servings (serving size: 1 baguette slice, 1 half-piece cheese, about 2½ tablespoons tuna, 2 tablespoons pickled vegetables, about 2 olives, ¼ ounce ham, and 1 tablespoon mayonnaise mixture).

prep: 10 minutes • **cook:** 12 minutes

SWISS CHARD AND CANNELLINI BEAN BRUSCHETTA

POINTS value:
4

exchanges:
2 starch
1 fat

per serving:
Calories 223
Fat 8g (saturated fat 1.4g)
Protein 5.8g
Carbohydrate 32.6g
Fiber 4.2g
Cholesterol 1mg
Iron 1.9mg
Sodium 374mg
Calcium 53mg

> *Bruschetta*
> *(broo-SKEH-tah),*
> *grilled garlic*
> *bread, becomes a*
> *healthy appetizer*
> *when topped with*
> *Swiss chard and*
> *beans.*

1   garlic clove
12   (¼-inch-thick) slices diagonally cut Italian or French bread baguette
Olive oil–flavored cooking spray
1   cup drained canned cannellini beans or other white beans, rinsed
1   tablespoon fresh lemon juice
¼   teaspoon freshly ground black pepper
⅛   teaspoon dried oregano
⅛   teaspoon dried thyme
⅛   teaspoon dried marjoram
1   tablespoon plus 2 teaspoons olive oil, divided
6   Swiss chard leaves, trimmed and thinly sliced
2   teaspoons balsamic vinegar
2   tablespoons finely grated fresh Parmigiano-Reggiano cheese

1. Preheat oven to 350°.
2. Cut garlic clove in half. Coarsely chop 1 garlic half; set aside remaining half.
3. Coat bread slices with cooking spray; place on a baking sheet. Bake at 350° for 5 minutes on each side.
4. While bread bakes, place coarsely chopped garlic, beans, and next 5 ingredients in a food processor. Add 1 tablespoon olive oil; process until smooth.
5. Heat remaining 2 teaspoons oil in a large nonstick skillet over medium–high heat. Add Swiss chard; sauté 30 seconds or just until wilted. Remove from heat; toss with balsamic vinegar.
6. Preheat broiler.
7. Rub 1 side of each toasted bread slice with reserved cut side of garlic. Top with 1 tablespoon bean purée and a heaping tablespoon of Swiss chard. Sprinkle evenly with cheese. Broil 1 minute or until cheese melts. Yield: 6 servings (serving size: 2 bruschetta).

Cool Minted Milk, page 33

Stuffed Mushrooms, page 30

Crostini with Wilted Spinach, Tomato, and Fresh Mozzarella, page 25

Creamy Pesto-Cheese Spread,
page 16

prep: 20 minutes • **cook:** 5 minutes • **other:** 5 minutes

CROSTINI WITH WILTED SPINACH, TOMATO, AND FRESH MOZZARELLA

pictured on page 23

Throughout Italy and especially in Tuscany, little open-faced sandwiches (crostini) are popular as a café snack. Fresh mozzarella cheese can be found in the deli section of most grocery stores. It can be vacuum-sealed or packed in a liquid brine.

16 (½-inch-thick) slices Italian or French bread baguette
Olive oil–flavored cooking spray
1   tablespoon extravirgin olive oil
1   tablespoon minced garlic (3 cloves)
1   (6-ounce) package baby spinach, coarsely chopped
½   teaspoon freshly ground black pepper
¼   teaspoon salt
1¼ cups finely chopped seeded plum tomato (about 3 large)
1   tablespoon balsamic vinegar
4   ounces fresh mozzarella cheese, thinly sliced

1. Preheat oven to 400°.
2. Coat bread slices with cooking spray; place on a baking sheet. Bake at 400° for 5 minutes or until lightly toasted; set aside.
3. While bread bakes, heat oil in a large nonstick skillet over medium-high heat. Add garlic; sauté 1 minute or until lightly browned. Add spinach, pepper, and salt, and sauté 30 seconds or until spinach wilts. Place spinach mixture in a bowl. Chill 5 minutes to quickly cool. Stir in tomato and vinegar. Top each bread slice evenly with cheese and about 2 tablespoons spinach mixture. Serve immediately. Yield: 8 servings (serving size: 2 crostini).

POINTS value:
4

exchanges:
1½ starch
1 vegetable
½ medium-fat meat
1 fat

per serving:
Calories 223
Fat 8.5g (saturated fat 2.9g)
Protein 6.5g
Carbohydrate 31g
Fiber 3.5g
Cholesterol 11mg
Iron 1.6mg
Sodium 341mg
Calcium 105mg

CROSTINI WITH MUSHROOM SPREAD AND RICOTTA SALATA

Because of its abundance of sheep, Sicily is well-known for its sheep's milk cheeses, such as ricotta salata. We fell in love with this dry, salted cheese that contributes a sharp, tangy flavor to the crostini.

POINTS value:
3

exchanges:
1 starch
1 vegetable
1 fat

per serving:
Calories 130
Fat 4.3g (saturated fat 0.8g)
Protein 3.6g
Carbohydrate 20.3g
Fiber 2g
Cholesterol 1mg
Iron 0.8mg
Sodium 248mg
Calcium 10mg

24 (½-inch-thick) slices diagonally cut Italian or French bread baguette
Olive oil–flavored cooking spray
2 (8-ounce) packages presliced mushrooms
4 teaspoons olive oil, divided
½ cup finely chopped shallots
2 garlic cloves, minced
½ teaspoon salt
2 tablespoons chopped fresh basil
2 tablespoons chopped fresh parsley
¼ teaspoon freshly ground black pepper
3 tablespoons crumbled ricotta salata or feta cheese
½ cup fresh basil leaves, cut into thin strips

1. Preheat oven to 375°.
2. Coat bread slices with cooking spray; place on baking sheets. Bake at 375° for 10 minutes or until toasted.
3. While bread bakes, place mushrooms in a food processor, and pulse 10 times or until finely chopped. Heat 1 teaspoon oil in a large nonstick skillet over medium-high heat. Add shallots and garlic, and sauté 1 minute. Add mushrooms and salt; cook 18 to 20 minutes or until liquid evaporates, stirring often. Remove from heat, and stir in remaining 1 tablespoon oil, 2 tablespoons chopped basil, parsley, and pepper. Spoon about 2½ teaspoons mushroom mixture evenly over each crostini. Sprinkle evenly with cheese and basil strips. Yield: 12 servings (serving size: 2 crostini).

Goat Cheese and Spinach Appetizer Pizza

Tradition would have you crush the fennel seeds with a mortar and pestle to release their licorice flavor, but a meat mallet or rolling pin will work just as well. Place the seeds in a small zip-top plastic bag. Wrap the plastic bag in a thin kitchen towel, and pound until the seeds are crushed. When cut into 8 slices, this cheesy pizza becomes a vegetarian entrée with a **POINTS** value of 4 per serving.

4	ounces goat cheese with garlic and herbs
2	cups thinly sliced fresh spinach leaves
½	cup part-skim ricotta cheese
½	teaspoon fennel seeds, crushed
¼	teaspoon freshly ground black pepper
1	(12-inch) thin Italian cheese-flavored pizza crust (such as Boboli)
1	cup drained chopped oil-packed sun-dried tomato halves (about 12 halves)
2	tablespoons grated Parmesan cheese
¼	teaspoon freshly ground black pepper

1. Preheat oven to 450°.

2. Combine first 5 ingredients in a medium bowl; stir until well blended. Spread cheese mixture evenly over crust, leaving a ½-inch border. Top with tomatoes, Parmesan cheese, and ¼ teaspoon pepper. Place on a baking sheet, and bake at 450° for 8 to 10 minutes or until browned and bubbly. Cut into 12 wedges. Yield: 12 servings (serving size: 1 wedge).

POINTS value:
3

exchanges:
½ starch
1 vegetable
1 medium-fat meat

per serving:
Calories 122
Fat 5g (saturated fat 2.3g)
Protein 6g
Carbohydrate 13.2g
Fiber 0.7g
Cholesterol 8mg
Iron 1.2mg
Sodium 209mg
Calcium 91mg

Asparagus Frittata

POINTS value:
3

exchanges:
½ starch
½ vegetable
1 medium-fat meat

per serving:
Calories 128
Fat 6.5g (saturated fat 2.2g)
Protein 7.9g
Carbohydrate 10.1g
Fiber 1.1g
Cholesterol 112mg
Iron 1mg
Sodium 480mg
Calcium 77mg

1	teaspoon salt
1½	ounces uncooked thin spaghetti, broken in half
4	large eggs
2	large egg whites
2	tablespoons water or 1% low-fat milk
½	teaspoon salt
¼	teaspoon black pepper
½	pound thin asparagus spears, trimmed
2	teaspoons olive oil
2	teaspoons butter
1	cup sliced mushrooms, coarsely chopped
½	cup chopped onion
1	teaspoon minced garlic
2	tablespoons chopped fresh basil
2	teaspoons chopped fresh oregano
⅓	cup shredded Asiago or Parmesan cheese
1	cup bottled or homemade marinara sauce (recipe on page 126)

1. Bring 6 cups water and 1 teaspoon salt to a boil; add pasta, and boil 6 minutes or until almost tender.

2. While pasta cooks, combine 4 eggs and next 4 ingredients in a medium bowl; stir well with a whisk. Set aside.

3. Cut asparagus into 1½-inch pieces. Place oil and butter in an ovenproof 10-inch nonstick skillet, and place over medium-high heat until butter melts. Add asparagus, and sauté 2 minutes. Remove asparagus from pan. Add mushrooms, onion, and garlic; sauté 3 minutes or until onion is tender and liquid evaporates. Remove pan from heat. Add asparagus. Drain pasta, and add to vegetables in pan. Stir in chopped basil and oregano.

4. Pour egg mixture over vegetables and pasta in pan. Place over medium heat. Cover and cook 8 minutes or until top is almost set (do not stir). Sprinkle with cheese.

5. Preheat broiler.

6. Broil 2 minutes or until golden. Cut into wedges. Serve with marinara. Yield: 8 servings (serving size: 1 wedge and 2 tablespoons marinara).

ROASTED ASPARAGUS WITH PROSCIUTTO

Prosciutto, a salt-cured, air-dried ham, adds a boost of flavor to this unique appetizer. Serve this dish warm or at room temperature. Don't save the recipe just for cocktail parties; serve it any night of the week as a side dish. You'll get four sides with a **POINTS** value of 0.

1   pound asparagus spears
Olive oil–flavored cooking spray
½   teaspoon grated fresh lemon rind
⅛   teaspoon crushed red pepper
⅛   teaspoon salt
⅛   teaspoon freshly ground black pepper
1   garlic clove, minced
¼   cup coarsely chopped prosciutto (about 1 ounce)

1. Preheat oven to 500°.
2. Snap off tough ends of asparagus. Place asparagus on a jelly-roll pan coated with cooking spray. Sprinkle with lemon rind and next 4 ingredients; coat asparagus generously with cooking spray, and toss well to coat. Sprinkle with prosciutto.
3. Bake at 500° for 8 to 10 minutes or until asparagus is crisp-tender. Yield: 6 servings (serving size: about 6 asparagus spears and 2 teaspoons prosciutto).

POINTS value:
0

exchange:
1 vegetable

per serving:
Calories 27
Fat 0.6g (saturated fat 0.2g)
Protein 3.1g
Carbohydrate 3.5g
Fiber 1.6g
Cholesterol 3mg
Iron 1.7mg
Sodium 135mg
Calcium 20mg

STUFFED MUSHROOMS
pictured on page 22

Leftover bread is used by resourceful Italian cooks to make stuffing for vegetables and meats that will be served at another meal. Look for large button mushrooms suitable for stuffing.

POINTS value:
1

exchanges:
1 vegetable
½ fat

per serving:
Calories 48
Fat 2.9g (saturated fat 1.1g)
Protein 2.3g
Carbohydrate 3.8g
Fiber 0.6g
Cholesterol 5mg
Iron 0.4mg
Sodium 163mg
Calcium 33mg

1   (16-ounce) package large mushrooms
     (12 mushrooms)
¼   teaspoon salt
1   tablespoon butter
1   tablespoon olive oil
2   tablespoons finely chopped onion
1   garlic clove, minced
3   tablespoons dry white wine
⅓   cup Italian-seasoned breadcrumbs
¼   cup grated pecorino Romano cheese
2   tablespoons chopped fresh flat-leaf parsley
½   teaspoon freshly ground black pepper
Cooking spray

1. Preheat oven to 350°.

2. Remove stems from mushrooms; finely chop stems. Sprinkle salt evenly over mushrooms.

3. Melt butter in a large nonstick skillet over medium-high heat; add oil. Add mushroom stems, onion, and garlic; sauté 4 minutes or until onion is tender. Add wine; cook 2 minutes or until liquid evaporates. Remove from heat; stir in breadcrumbs and next 3 ingredients.

4. Spoon about 2 tablespoons stuffing mixture into each mushroom cap. Place mushrooms on a baking sheet coated with cooking spray; lightly coat each mushroom with cooking spray. Bake at 350° for 14 minutes or until mushrooms are tender and stuffing is lightly browned. Serve immediately. Yield: 12 servings (serving size: 1 mushroom).

CLAMS OREGANATA

Italians love leisurely multicourse meals, with a different wine served with each course. It's common to start the meal with seafood, such as this dish. It's impressive for guests, yet it's quick and simple to prepare.

24	littleneck, Manila, or cherrystone clams, scrubbed
¼	cup dry breadcrumbs
1	tablespoon chopped fresh oregano
1½	teaspoons chopped fresh mint
1	teaspoon fresh lemon juice
¼	teaspoon black pepper
⅛	teaspoon kosher salt or dash of table salt
1	garlic clove, minced
2	tablespoons extravirgin olive oil

POINTS value:
2

exchanges:
½ starch
1 very lean meat
½ fat

per serving:
Calories 90
Fat 4.3g (saturated fat 0.6g)
Protein 8.2g
Carbohydrate 4.4g
Fiber 0.3g
Cholesterol 20mg
Iron 8.7mg
Sodium 88mg
Calcium 39mg

1. Shuck clams, and discard top shells. Loosen meat from bottom shell, and arrange clams in shells on a jelly-roll pan.
2. Preheat broiler.
3. Combine breadcrumbs and next 6 ingredients in a small bowl. Slowly add olive oil, tossing with a fork until well blended (crumb mixture should be moist but not soggy).
4. Spoon ½ teaspoon crumb mixture onto each clam. Broil 5 to 10 minutes or until crumbs are lightly brown and clams are just cooked through. Serve warm. Yield: 8 servings (serving size: 3 clams).

Fresh Clams: When purchasing clams, choose shells that are clamped tightly shut. If the shell moves easily, the clam is probably dead and unsafe to eat. Store clams in an open bowl in the refrigerator, and use them as soon as possible. Do not store clams in a sealed plastic bag or on ice because they will die. To shuck (open) clams, place them in the freezer for 15 to 30 minutes. After briefly freezing the clams, let them stand at room temperature a few minutes to relax. Working over a bowl or sink, hold the clam securely in one hand, and insert a clam knife into the opening of the shell between the top and bottom halves. You may want to protect your hand with a towel. If you don't have a clam knife, you may use a thin, short, dull knife. Never use a sharp kitchen knife. Using the blade of the knife, cut through the hinge muscle, and open the shell. Carefully slide the knife between the clam and the shell to detach the meat.

BELLINIS

In 1948, a bartender with a love for white peaches invented the Bellini at Harry's Bar in Venice. While the original consisted of only white peach purée and sweet sparkling wine, the cocktail has taken many twists and turns over time. Instead of white peaches, we use readily available frozen peaches so that you can enjoy the beverage year-round. A light, fruity, sparkling wine, such as Asti spumante, tastes best with the sweet peach purée.

POINTS value:
1

exchanges:
½ starch
½ fruit

per serving:
Calories 75
Fat 0g (saturated fat 0g)
Protein 0.3g
Carbohydrate 12.3g
Fiber 0.5g
Cholesterol 0mg
Iron 0.2mg
Sodium 4mg
Calcium 3mg

1   cup frozen peach slices, thawed
1½   cups chilled peach nectar
1   tablespoon orange-flavored liqueur (such as Cointreau)
¾   cup chilled sweet sparkling white wine

1. Combine peach slices and nectar in a blender; process until very smooth. Add orange liqueur and sparkling wine, and stir gently. Serve immediately in champagne flutes or wine glasses. Yield: 6 servings (serving size: ½ cup).

Note: For a nonalcoholic version, omit sparkling wine and orange liqueur, and substitute ¾ cup chilled sparkling water, sparkling white grape juice, or ginger ale.

COOL MINTED MILK
pictured on page 21

Italians enjoy summertime while sipping this cool, refreshing beverage that's typically served in the afternoon. They make this drink with a mint-flavored syrup found in their grocery stores and markets. The mint-infused simple syrup that we've created for this beverage also tastes delicious in lemonade, tea, and hot chocolate.

½   cup chopped fresh mint
½   cup water
¼   cup sugar
8   cups 1% low-fat milk

1. Bring first 3 ingredients to a boil in a medium saucepan, stirring to dissolve sugar. Reduce heat; simmer 1 minute. Remove from heat; cover and cool completely.
2. Press mixture through a fine sieve over a bowl, reserving mint syrup; discard mint leaves.
3. Combine mint syrup and milk; stir well. Serve immediately. Yield: 8 servings (serving size: 1 cup).

Note: If you prefer to serve this beverage by the glass rather than by the pitcher, stir 4 teaspoons mint syrup into 1 cup milk.

POINTS value:
3

exchanges:
½ starch
1 low-fat milk

per serving:
Calories 130
Fat 2.7g (saturated fat 1.6g)
Protein 8.3g
Carbohydrate 18.5g
Fiber 0g
Cholesterol 10mg
Iron 0.5mg
Sodium 123mg
Calcium 319mg

CAPPUCCINO

When you think of Italy, you can't help but think of coffee, especially cappuccino, which is the national breakfast. Swirled with steamed milk and topped with a dollop of foam, this drink is named for its resemblance to the Capuchin monk's habit, which is light brown with a white hood. While it may sound like a special coffee-shop drink, cappuccino is quite easy to prepare. A balloon whisk is as fancy a gadget as you need to create the perfect froth on top.

POINTS value:
1

exchange:
½ low-fat milk

per serving:
Calories 46
Fat 1.1g (saturated fat 0.7g)
Protein 3g
Carbohydrate 5.8g
Fiber 0g
Cholesterol 4mg
Iron 0.2mg
Sodium 59mg
Calcium 114mg

¾ cup 1% low-fat milk
¾ cup hot brewed espresso
Ground cinnamon or nutmeg (optional)

1. Place milk in a small saucepan; cook over medium heat 2 minutes or until a thermometer registers between 140° and 160°, stirring constantly with a whisk. Remove from heat; whisk vigorously for 30 seconds or until foamy.
2. Divide milk (with froth) and brewed espresso equally between 2 mugs. Sprinkle with cinnamon or nutmeg, if desired. Yield: 2 servings (serving size: ¾ cup).

Note: If you don't own an espresso machine, look for instant espresso granules (such as Café Bustelo) in large supermarkets or specialty coffee shops. We used 2 teaspoons instant espresso granules in ¾ cup boiling water, but the espresso can be made stronger to suit your personal taste.

Desserts

CHERRIES IN CHIANTI WITH HONEYED MASCARPONE CREAM

POINTS value:
5

exchanges:
2 starch
1 fruit

per serving:
Calories 223
Fat 5.5g (saturated fat 2.9g)
Protein 2.8g
Carbohydrate 43.8g
Fiber 1.5g
Cholesterol 15mg
Iron 1.1mg
Sodium 34mg
Calcium 77mg

2   cups Chianti
1   (12-ounce) package frozen sweet dark cherries, thawed
½   cup packed light brown sugar
⅓   cup vanilla fat-free yogurt
¼   cup mascarpone cheese
2   tablespoons honey
Mint leaves (optional)

1. Combine first 3 ingredients in a medium saucepan; bring to a boil. Reduce heat slightly; simmer vigorously 20 minutes or until reduced to 1¼ cups. Pour cherry mixture into a bowl; cover and refrigerate 1 hour or until chilled.
2. Combine yogurt, mascarpone cheese, and honey in a small bowl; stir with a whisk until smooth. Cover and chill until ready to serve.
3. Divide cherry mixture evenly among 5 small dessert bowls; top each serving with mascarpone cream. Garnish with mint leaves, if desired. Yield: 5 servings (serving size: ¼ cup cherry mixture and 2 tablespoons cream).

Mascarpone: If you've ever tasted mascarpone, you've probably fallen in love with its soft, velvety texture and buttery-rich flavor. Mascarpone is produced when a culture is added to the heavy cream that's skimmed off cow's milk. Originating in the Lombardy region of southern Italy, mascarpone may have gotten its name from the local word for ricotta, *mascherpa*, since the two are similar in texture. Mascarpone is used primarily in desserts, but it also adds richness to pasta and savory dishes.

WARM FIGS WITH HONEY AND GORGONZOLA

Because figs grow abundantly throughout the country, they may appear on the Italian table as part of the antipasto or as an entrée. And they often steal the show as a dessert. You'll see why when you taste this combination of succulent figs, walnuts, and Gorgonzola cheese drizzled with warm honey and sweet wine.

⅓ cup honey
2 tablespoons riesling or other slightly sweet white wine
12 ripe fresh figs (about 1 pound), halved
Cooking spray
½ cup (2 ounces) crumbled Gorgonzola cheese
1½ teaspoons ground walnuts

1. Preheat oven to 325°.
2. Combine honey and wine in a medium bowl; stir well. Add figs, and toss gently to coat. Spoon figs and honey mixture into an 8-inch square baking dish coated with cooking spray. Bake at 325° for 25 minutes or until thoroughly heated.
3. Place 4 fig halves on each of 6 dessert plates; drizzle warm honey mixture evenly over figs. Sprinkle 4 teaspoons cheese and ¼ teaspoon walnuts over each serving. Serve immediately. Yield: 6 servings.

Note: You may substitute white grape juice for the riesling, if desired.

***POINTS* value:**
3

exchanges:
1 starch
1½ fruit

per serving:
Calories 168
Fat 3.3g (saturated fat 2.1g)
Protein 2.9g
Carbohydrate 35.2g
Fiber 3.3g
Cholesterol 8mg
Iron 0.5mg
Sodium 130mg
Calcium 88mg

Fresh Figs: Fresh figs are available twice a year. The first crop is available from June through July; the second crop begins early in September and lasts through mid-October. The figs from the first crop are larger and more flavorful than those from the second. Figs are extremely perishable, so you should either use them soon after they're purchased or store them in the refrigerator for no more than two to three days.

AMARETTI-CRUSTED PEACHES

Baked almond-filled peach halves are a favorite summertime dessert. The almond flavor and the crunch of the amaretti cookies perfectly complement the sweet, juicy fresh peaches. Look for macaroon-type amaretti cookies in Italian markets, gourmet stores, and large supermarkets.

POINTS value:
2

exchanges:
1 starch
½ fruit

per serving:
Calories 125
Fat 3g (saturated fat 1.2g)
Protein 2.5g
Carbohydrate 23.7g
Fiber 1.4g
Cholesterol 5mg
Iron 0.5mg
Sodium 67mg
Calcium 4mg

1 cup amaretti cookie crumbs (about 32 cookies)
4 teaspoons sugar
4 teaspoons butter, melted
1 tablespoon apple juice
4 fresh peaches (about 1¾ pounds), halved and pitted
Cooking spray

1. Preheat oven to 375°.
2. Combine first 4 ingredients in a small bowl; toss with a fork until well blended.
3. Place peach halves, cut sides up, in a 13 x 9–inch baking dish coated with cooking spray. Spoon 2 heaping tablespoons cookie mixture into center of each peach half.
4. Bake, uncovered, at 375° for 30 to 35 minutes or until peaches are tender and cookie mixture is lightly browned (shield with foil to prevent overbrowning, if necessary). Yield: 8 servings (serving size: 1 peach half).

Note: Substitute 1 cup gingersnap or biscotti crumbs for the amaretti cookie crumbs, if desired. If fresh peaches are out of season, substitute drained canned peach halves in light syrup.

GRILLED PEACHES WITH ALMOND CREAM

Almond is a favorite flavoring for Italian desserts, and it pairs beautifully with sugary-sweet peaches in this classic combo. Use peaches that are nice and ripe but still firm so they will hold up on the grill.

4	medium firm ripe peaches (about 1½ pounds), halved and pitted
3	tablespoons amaretto (almond-flavored liqueur)
¼	cup sliced almonds, toasted and divided
2	tablespoons sugar
1	(8-ounce) block ⅓-less-fat cream cheese, softened
1	teaspoon vanilla extract

Cooking spray

1. Prepare grill.

2. Combine peaches and amaretto in a large bowl, tossing gently to coat. Let stand 15 minutes.

3. While peaches stand, place 2 tablespoons almonds and sugar in a food processor; process 3 minutes or until a paste forms. Add cream cheese and vanilla; process until smooth.

4. Remove peaches from bowl, reserving amaretto. Place peaches, cut sides down, on grill rack coated with cooking spray; brush peaches with reserved amaretto. Grill 5 to 6 minutes on each side or until tender, basting occasionally with amaretto. Place peach halves on dessert plates; spoon 2 tablespoons almond cream into center of each peach half, and sprinkle evenly with remaining 2 tablespoons almonds. Serve warm. Yield: 8 servings (serving size: 1 peach half, 2 tablespoons almond cream, and ¾ teaspoon almonds).

Note: You may substitute ¼ teaspoon almond extract plus 3 tablespoons water for the amaretto, if desired.

POINTS value:
3

exchanges:
1 fruit
2 fat

per serving:
Calories 149
Fat 8.3g (saturated fat 4.2g)
Protein 4.5g
Carbohydrate 12.4g
Fiber 1.6g
Cholesterol 20mg
Iron 0mg
Sodium 127mg
Calcium 20mg

Warm Hazelnut Pears with Sweet Mascarpone Cream

Used in a variety of Italian confections, toasted hazelnuts add crunch and a pleasant contrast to the creamy mascarpone sauce and warm, soft pears. If your pears are very ripe, you will not need to cook them quite as long. Watch them closely so they don't overcook. They should be tender but still crisp in the center.

POINTS value:
6

exchanges:
1½ starch
1 fruit
2 fat

per serving:
Calories 326
Fat 9.2g (saturated fat 4.4g)
Protein 3.8g
Carbohydrate 52.9g
Fiber 5.2g
Cholesterol 25mg
Iron 0.5mg
Sodium 51mg
Calcium 71mg

½ cup fat-free ricotta cheese
¼ cup mascarpone cheese
2 tablespoons granulated sugar
½ teaspoon vanilla extract
2 tablespoons butter
4 large ripe pears (about 1¾ pounds), peeled, cored, and sliced
¼ cup Frangelico (hazelnut-flavored liqueur)
1 tablespoon brown sugar
5 teaspoons chopped hazelnuts, toasted

1. Combine first 4 ingredients in a small bowl; stir with a whisk until smooth.
2. Melt butter in a large nonstick skillet over medium-high heat. Add pears, and sauté 10 minutes or until tender. Add Frangelico and brown sugar, and cook 1 minute, stirring constantly.
3. Divide warm pear mixture evenly among 5 dessert plates; drizzle with mascarpone cream, and sprinkle with hazelnuts. Yield: 5 servings (serving size: about ½ cup pear mixture, about 3 tablespoons cream, and 1 teaspoon hazelnuts).

A Toast to Nuts: One of the best ways to bring out the flavor in nuts is to toast them. Heating helps release flavor compounds that make for a richer, more intensely nutty taste. To toast hazelnuts, place them in a shallow pan or on a baking sheet, and bake at 350° for 15 minutes or until the nuts are fragrant, stirring once. (Or quickly toast them in a skillet over medium-high heat.) Turn nuts out onto a towel. Roll up the towel, and rub the hazelnuts to remove the skins.

**Raspberry-Chocolate Torte,
page 56**

Affogato, page 63,
and Lemon Affogato, page 64

Panforte, page 58

Panna Cotta with Fresh Berries, page 48

BALSAMIC STRAWBERRIES OVER POUND CAKE

Italians love simple desserts where fruit is the star, and this one is a perfect example.
A splash of sweet balsamic vinegar enhances the flavor of the strawberries.
Toast the cake slices before topping them with fruit, if desired.

1   tablespoon butter
2   tablespoons sugar
1   tablespoon balsamic vinegar
2   cups fresh strawberries, halved
1   teaspoon grated fresh orange rind
1   (10-ounce) package light frozen pound cake, thawed
      and cut into 12 slices

1. Melt butter in a large nonstick skillet over medium-high heat. Stir in sugar and vinegar; cook 1 minute or until sugar dissolves and mixture is slightly thick. Stir in strawberries and orange rind, and cook 3 minutes or until strawberries are tender. Serve warm strawberry mixture over cake slices. Yield: 6 servings (serving size: 2 cake slices and about ¼ cup strawberry mixture).

POINTS value:
4

exchanges:
2 starch
½ fruit

per serving:
Calories 186
Fat 4.7g (saturated fat 1.9g)
Protein 2.4g
Carbohydrate 34.8g
Fiber 1.8g
Cholesterol 5mg
Iron 2.7mg
Sodium 208mg
Calcium 24mg

prep: 6 minutes • cook: 2 minutes

PEPPERED STRAWBERRIES WITH AMARETTO AND ICE CREAM

Strawberries grow bountifully outside of Rome, where they cover the hillsides surrounding volcanic Lake Nemi. Because of this, these berries are often incorporated into simple Italian desserts. It may seem odd to the American palate to add black pepper to strawberries, but these two ingredients are natural food partners. The spicy pepper accentuates the flavor of the sweet, juicy strawberries.

POINTS value:
4

exchanges:
2 starch
½ fruit
1 fat

per serving:
Calories 214
Fat 6.2g (saturated fat 3.4g)
Protein 3.6g
Carbohydrate 35.7g
Fiber 1.7g
Cholesterol 6mg
Iron 0.6mg
Sodium 89mg
Calcium 83mg

¼   cup firmly packed light brown sugar
2   tablespoons light butter
2   tablespoons amaretto (almond-flavored liqueur)
½   teaspoon freshly ground black pepper
2½ cups sliced fresh strawberries (about 1 pound)
2½ cups vanilla light ice cream

1. Combine first 4 ingredients in a small saucepan; cook over medium heat 2 minutes or until sugar dissolves. Stir in strawberries; remove from heat. Serve immediately over ice cream. Yield: 5 servings (serving size: ½ cup strawberries and ½ cup ice cream).

Note: You may substitute ¼ teaspoon almond extract plus 2 tablespoons water for the amaretto, if desired.

FRESH FRUIT WITH CANNOLI CREAM

In traditional cannoli, a well-known Sicilian dessert, pastry tubes ("pipes") are deep-fried and filled with sweet ricotta cream. We eliminated the time-consuming pastry, greatly reducing the calories and fat. But we kept the best part—the cannoli cream—and spooned it over fresh fruit.

⅓   cup part-skim ricotta cheese
2½ tablespoons tub-style light cream cheese, softened
2½ tablespoons orange marmalade
⅛   teaspoon vanilla extract
¾   cup frozen fat-free whipped topping, thawed
1½ cups sliced fresh strawberries
1   cup fresh blueberries
2   medium kiwifruit, peeled and diced
1   tablespoon grated semisweet chocolate
2   tablespoons sliced almonds, lightly toasted

1. Combine first 4 ingredients in a large bowl. Fold whipped topping into ricotta mixture.
2. Combine strawberries, blueberries, and kiwifruit in a bowl, toss gently.
3. Spoon about ½ cup fruit into each of 6 dessert dishes; top each serving with 3 tablespoons cannoli cream, ½ teaspoon grated semisweet chocolate, and 1 teaspoon sliced almonds. Yield: 6 servings.

POINTS value:
2

exchanges:
½ starch
1 fruit
½ fat

per serving:
Calories 123
Fat 3.5g (saturated fat 1.5g)
Protein 3.3g
Carbohydrate 20g
Fiber 2.2g
Cholesterol 8mg
Iron 0.4mg
Sodium 51mg
Calcium 50mg

PANNA COTTA WITH FRESH BERRIES
pictured on page 44

Our version of *panna cotta* is sweet, creamy, and delicious—with only a fraction of the fat. It's quicker than the traditional recipe because you skip the molding process and chill it in your prettiest glass stemware instead. You can make the panna cotta a day in advance and keep it in the refrigerator, which makes it ideal for dinner parties.

POINTS value:
4

exchanges:
3 starch

per serving:
Calories 222
Fat 2.8g (saturated fat 1.7g)
Protein 7.9g
Carbohydrate 41.1g
Fiber 1g
Cholesterol 18mg
Iron 0.1mg
Sodium 98mg
Calcium 221mg

> ***Panna cotta***
> *(PAHN-nah KOH-tah), or "cooked cream," is a tra-ditionally molded and chilled dessert that's popular through-out Italy.*

1	envelope unflavored gelatin
2	cups whole milk, divided
1	tablespoon sugar
⅛	teaspoon ground cinnamon
1	cup fat-free sweetened condensed milk, divided
¼	teaspoon vanilla extract
⅛	teaspoon almond extract
½	cup fresh blueberries
½	cup fresh raspberries

1. Sprinkle gelatin over 1 cup whole milk in a small saucepan; let stand 10 minutes. Cook over medium–low heat 5 minutes or until gelatin dissolves, stirring constantly with a whisk. Increase heat to medium, and add sugar and cinnamon; cook, stirring constantly, until sugar dissolves, about 2 minutes. Remove from heat; gradually stir in remaining 1 cup whole milk, 1 cup sweetened condensed milk, vanilla, and almond extract. Pour ½ cup panna cotta into each of 6 stemmed glasses; cover and chill overnight.
2. Spoon about 1 tablespoon blueberries and about 1 tablespoon raspberries over each serving. Let stand at room temperature 5 minutes before serving. Yield: 6 servings.

ZABAGLIONE WITH SEASONAL FRUIT

When we prepared the *zabaglione,* we found that a wide metal bowl placed over a pan of simmering water produced greater volume than a double boiler.

⅓ cup sweet Marsala wine
¼ cup sugar
4 large egg yolks
7 ripe fresh figs (about 10 ounces), quartered
2 cups mixed fresh berries (such as blueberries, raspberries, blackberries, and sliced strawberries)
1 cup fat-free canned refrigerated whipped topping (such as Reddi-wip)
Mint sprigs (optional)

1. Add water to a large saucepan to a depth of 1 inch; bring water to a simmer over high heat. Reduce heat until water is barely simmering and producing steam.
2. Combine Marsala, sugar, and egg yolks in a large metal bowl (bowl should be large enough to sit on top of saucepan but not in saucepan); beat with a mixer at medium speed until well blended. Place bowl over saucepan of simmering water; beat egg mixture 4 minutes or until thick and pale and thermometer registers 160° (mixture will hold its shape for a few moments when beaters are removed from bowl).
3. Spoon ⅔ cup zabaglione into 4 shallow rimmed soup bowls; top with 7 fig quarters, ½ cup berries, and ¼ cup whipped topping. Garnish with mint, if desired. Yield: 4 servings.

Note: Substitute 2 cups sliced peeled peaches or nectarines for the figs, if desired.

***POINTS* value:**
4

exchanges:
1½ starch
1 fruit
½ fat

per serving:
Calories 198
Fat 4.9g (saturated fat 1.6g)
Protein 3.9g
Carbohydrate 36.8g
Fiber 4.8g
Cholesterol 205mg
Iron 1.2mg
Sodium 11mg
Calcium 61mg

Zabaglione (zah-bahl-YOH-nay) is a classic Venetian dessert made of egg yolks, sugar, and sweet Marsala wine that's usually served warm over fresh fruit or plain cakes.

ZUPPA INGLESE

This chilled dessert is traditionally made with layers of rum-soaked cake, creamy pudding, whipped cream, and candied fruit or almonds. We created individual servings by layering the ingredients in a variety of glasses and stemware.

POINTS value:
4

exchanges:
2 starch
½ fat

per serving:
Calories 195
Fat 2.2g (saturated fat 0.4g)
Protein 7.9g
Carbohydrate 29.8g
Fiber 1.1g
Cholesterol 28mg
Iron 0.5mg
Sodium 444mg
Calcium 228mg

> ***Zuppa Inglese***
> *(ZOO-puh ihn-GLAY-zay) literally translates as "English soup."*

1   (1.4-ounce) package sugar-free chocolate instant pudding mix
1   (1-ounce) package sugar-free vanilla instant pudding mix
4   cups fat-free milk, divided
1   teaspoon grated fresh orange rind
¼   teaspoon almond extract
2   tablespoons dark rum
2   tablespoons amaretto (almond-flavored liqueur)
1   (3-ounce) package cakelike ladyfingers, split
6   tablespoons frozen fat-free whipped topping, thawed
2   tablespoons slivered almonds, toasted

1. Prepare chocolate and vanilla pudding mixes according to package directions, using 2 cups of milk in each. Stir orange rind into vanilla pudding. Stir almond extract into chocolate pudding.

2. Combine rum and amaretto in a small bowl.

3. Tear 1 ladyfinger half into pieces, and place in bottom of a 6-ounce wine glass; drizzle with ½ teaspoon rum mixture. Top with about 2 tablespoons vanilla pudding. Tear another ladyfinger half into pieces, and place over vanilla-pudding layer; drizzle with ½ teaspoon rum mixture, and top with about 2 tablespoons chocolate pudding. Repeat layers, ending with chocolate pudding. Repeat procedure with remaining ingredients and 5 wine glasses. Cover and chill at least 2 hours.

4. Spoon 1 tablespoon whipped topping onto each parfait; sprinkle each with 1 teaspoon almonds. Yield: 6 servings.

Note: You may substitute ½ teaspoon rum extract plus 2 tablespoons orange juice for the rum. You may substitute ¼ teaspoon almond extract plus 2 tablespoons water for the amaretto, if desired.

ARBORIO RICE PUDDING WITH SAFFRON

Our staff gave this rice pudding our highest rating. Italian short-grain rice creates a wonderfully creamy texture. Saffron lends an aromatic flavor and a rich, golden color to the dessert.

6   cups 1% low-fat milk, divided
1   cup uncooked Arborio rice
⅔   cup sugar
½   teaspoon salt
⅛   teaspoon saffron threads
¼   teaspoon ground cinnamon
½   cup golden raisins
1   teaspoon vanilla extract
Cinnamon sticks (optional)

1. Combine 3 cups milk, rice, sugar, salt, saffron, and ¼ teaspoon ground cinnamon in a large glass bowl. Microwave at HIGH 9 minutes.

2. Stir in remaining 3 cups milk. Microwave at HIGH 28 to 30 minutes or until rice is tender and pudding is creamy and slightly thick (pudding will continue to thicken after cooking as it stands), stirring every few minutes to prevent mixture from bubbling over.

3. Stir in raisins and vanilla. Serve warm or chilled. Garnish with cinnamon sticks, if desired. Yield: 9 servings (serving size: ½ cup).

Note: We tested with an 1,100-watt microwave. All microwaves cook differently, so use the texture of the rice and pudding as your guide to determine when it is done, not the exact time.

POINTS **value:**
4

exchanges:
2 starch
½ fruit

per serving:
Calories 187
Fat 1.8g (saturated fat 1.1g)
Protein 6.3g
Carbohydrate 37.1g
Fiber 0.5g
Cholesterol 7mg
Iron 0.3mg
Sodium 214mg
Calcium 205mg

TIRAMISÙ
pictured on page 1

Brandy and espresso–soaked ladyfingers are joined with an Italian meringue, mascarpone, and sweet Marsala wine to make a heavenly combination. Make this ahead; it chills in the refrigerator overnight.

***POINTS* value:**
5

exchanges:
1½ starch
2 fat

per serving:
Calories 216
Fat 10g (saturated fat 5.3g)
Protein 4.2g
Carbohydrate 24.7g
Fiber 0.2g
Cholesterol 40mg
Iron 0.4mg
Sodium 93mg
Calcium 58mg

Tiramisù (tih-ruh-mee-SOO) means "pick me up." Try one taste of this dessert, and you'll understand why.

¼ cup water
¼ cup brandy
2 tablespoons instant espresso granules or 4 tablespoons instant coffee
1 (3-ounce) package cakelike ladyfingers, split
1 cup sugar
4 large egg whites
1 (8.8-ounce) carton mascarpone cheese
1 cup plain fat-free yogurt
¼ cup sweet Marsala wine
1 teaspoon instant espresso granules
1½ teaspoons unsweetened cocoa

1. Combine first 3 ingredients; stir well. Place 2 ladyfinger halves in bottom of each of 12 (4-ounce) coffee cups. Brush brandy mixture evenly over ladyfingers. Set aside.
2. Add water to a large saucepan to a depth of 1 inch; bring to a simmer over medium heat. Reduce heat to medium-low. Combine sugar and egg whites in a large metal bowl (bowl should be large enough to sit on top of saucepan but not in saucepan). Place bowl over saucepan of simmering water; cook 21 minutes or until thermometer registers 160°, stirring constantly. Remove bowl from simmering water; beat egg mixture with a mixer at high speed 8 minutes or until stiff peaks form.
3. Beat mascarpone and next 3 ingredients in a large bowl at medium speed until blended and smooth. Gently fold in egg mixture. Divide mixture evenly among coffee cups lined with ladyfingers. Sift cocoa evenly over tops of desserts. Cover and chill at least 8 hours. Yield: 12 servings (serving size: about ½ cup).

AMARETTO-RICOTTA CHEESECAKE

Italian cheesecakes are made with ricotta cheese, producing a firm and creamy yet slightly granular texture. Sweet amaretto flavors the filling of this luscious cake, while almond biscotti produces a deliciously nutty crust.

6	almond biscotti (about 7 ounces)
¼	cup sugar
1	large egg white
1	(15-ounce) carton part-skim ricotta cheese
¾	cup (6 ounces) ⅓-less-fat cream cheese, softened
⅔	cup sugar
¼	cup amaretto (almond-flavored liqueur)
2	tablespoons all-purpose flour
1	large egg
1	large egg white

1. Preheat oven to 375°.

2. Place biscotti in a food processor; process until fine crumbs form to yield 1⅓ cups. Add ¼ cup sugar; process until blended. Add 1 egg white, and process until blended. Press crumb mixture into bottom and 1 inch up sides of an 8-inch springform pan.

3. Bake at 375° for 15 minutes. Cool slightly in pan on a wire rack. Reduce oven temperature to 350°.

4. Combine ricotta and next 3 ingredients in a large bowl; beat with a mixer at medium speed until smooth. Add flour, egg, and 1 egg white, beating just until blended. Pour batter into prepared crust. Gently tap on counter to remove air bubbles.

5. Bake at 350° for 45 minutes. Remove from oven, and carefully run a knife around outside edge of cake. Cool completely in pan on wire rack. Cover and chill overnight. Yield: 12 servings (serving size: 1 slice).

Note: Before chilling cheesecake, place a paper towel over pan before covering with foil. This will catch the condensation that forms around the cheesecake while it's in the refrigerator. You may substitute ½ teaspoon almond extract plus ¼ cup water for the amaretto, if desired.

POINTS value:
5

exchanges:
2 starch
1½ fat

per serving:
Calories 226
Fat 8.8g (saturated fat 4.9g)
Protein 7.3g
Carbohydrate 28.2g
Fiber 0.5g
Cholesterol 51mg
Iron 0.5mg
Sodium 145mg
Calcium 109mg

ITALIAN ALMOND CAKE

Cornmeal, which was introduced to Italy via the Orient, is commonly used in baked goods like this almond cake and the well-known polenta cake (recipe on facing page). This cake has a flavorful addition of orange juice–soaked raisins. Top each slice with 1 tablespoon fat-free whipped topping and 2 tablespoons fresh raspberries for a stunning presentation without changing the **POINTS** value.

POINTS value:
6

exchanges:
2 starch
½ fruit
2 fat

per serving:
Calories 264
Fat 10.4g (saturated fat 4.7g)
Protein 4.8g
Carbohydrate 39.8g
Fiber 1.2g
Cholesterol 120mg
Iron 1.7mg
Sodium 234mg
Calcium 104mg

¼ cup orange juice
½ cup raisins
½ cup yellow cornmeal
½ cup sifted cake flour
1 teaspoon baking powder
¼ cup butter, softened
¼ cup marzipan (almond paste), cut into small pieces
½ teaspoon vanilla extract
1¼ cups powdered sugar, sifted
2 large eggs
2 large egg yolks
¼ cup low-fat vanilla yogurt
Cooking spray
1½ teaspoons powdered sugar

1. Preheat oven to 350°.
2. Microwave juice in a small bowl at HIGH 30 seconds or until hot. Add raisins. Let stand 10 minutes; drain.
3. Combine cornmeal, flour, and baking powder in a bowl.
4. Combine butter, marzipan, and vanilla in a large bowl; beat with a mixer at medium speed until very smooth. Gradually add 1¼ cups powdered sugar, beating until light and fluffy. Add eggs and egg yolks, 1 at a time, beating well after each addition. Add cornmeal mixture and yogurt, beating until blended. Stir in raisins. Pour batter into an 8-inch round cake pan coated with cooking spray.
5. Bake at 350° for 30 minutes or until a wooden pick inserted in center comes out clean. Cool in pan 10 minutes on a wire rack. Remove from pan; cool completely on a wire rack. Sprinkle with 1½ teaspoons powdered sugar. Yield: 8 servings.

POLENTA CAKE WITH AMARETTO ORANGES

½ cup slivered almonds, toasted
1 cup sugar
¼ cup butter, softened
3 large eggs
1 teaspoon grated fresh lemon rind
¼ cup fresh lemon juice
1¼ cups instant polenta
½ teaspoon salt
½ teaspoon baking powder
Cooking spray
2 large navel oranges (about 1¾ pounds)
¼ cup amaretto (almond-flavored liqueur)
1 tablespoon sugar

1. Preheat oven to 375°.
2. Place toasted almonds in a food processor, and process until ground; set aside.
3. Place 1 cup sugar and butter in a large bowl; beat with a mixer at medium speed until fluffy. Add eggs, 1 at a time, beating well after each addition. Stir in lemon rind and juice.
4. Combine ground almonds, polenta, salt, and baking powder in a large bowl. Add egg mixture, and stir until well blended. Pour batter into an 8-inch springform pan coated with cooking spray.
5. Bake at 375° for 25 minutes or until a wooden pick inserted in center comes out clean. Cool completely in pan on a wire rack.
6. While cake cools, cut peel and pith away from oranges using a sharp knife. Cut oranges crosswise into ¼-inch slices; cut each slice into quarters. Combine oranges, amaretto, and 1 tablespoon sugar, stirring gently until sugar dissolves.
7. Cut cake into 8 wedges. Spoon oranges and syrup over cake. Yield: 8 servings (serving size: 1 cake slice and ¼ cup orange mixture).

Note: Substitute ¼ cup orange juice, ¼ teaspoon almond extract, and 1 tablespoon sugar for the amaretto, if desired.

POINTS **value:**
7

exchanges:
3 starch
½ fruit
2 fat

per serving:
Calories 363
Fat 11.1g (saturated fat 4.5g)
Protein 6.3g
Carbohydrate 53.5g
Fiber 4.7g
Cholesterol 94mg
Iron 0.8mg
Sodium 244mg
Calcium 76mg

RASPBERRY–CHOCOLATE TORTES
pictured on page 41

POINTS value:
4

exchanges:
2½ starch
½ fat

per serving:
Calories 216
Fat 6.6g (saturated fat 3.8g)
Protein 4.3g
Carbohydrate 37.9g
Fiber 2g
Cholesterol 14mg
Iron 1.4mg
Sodium 103mg
Calcium 25mg

Cooking spray
2   tablespoons unsweetened cocoa
¼   cup butter
¼   cup seedless raspberry preserves (such as Dickinson's)
¼   cup fat-free half-and-half
½   cup unsweetened cocoa
¾   cup granulated sugar
¾   cup egg substitute
¼   cup all-purpose flour
1   teaspoon vanilla extract
3   tablespoons fat-free hot fudge topping
2½   tablespoons seedless raspberry preserves
1½   teaspoons water
1½   tablespoons powdered sugar

1. Preheat oven to 450°.
2. Coat 9 muffin cups with cooking spray, and dust with 2 tablespoons cocoa. Set aside.
3. Melt butter in a small saucepan over low heat. Add ¼ cup preserves and half-and-half, stirring with a whisk until preserves melt. Remove from heat; add ½ cup cocoa, stirring until smooth.
4. Combine granulated sugar and egg substitute in medium bowl; beat with a mixer at high speed 5 minutes. Gradually add chocolate mixture to egg substitute mixture, beating until smooth. Add flour, beating until blended. Stir in vanilla.
5. Divide batter evenly among prepared muffin cups. Spoon 1 teaspoon fudge topping into center of each torte.
6. Bake at 450° for 8 to 10 minutes or until edges are set and center is soft. Cool 2 minutes. Run a thin, flexible knife around edge of each muffin cup. Carefully invert tortes onto a baking sheet; transfer to dessert plates.
7. Combine 2½ tablespoons preserves and 1½ teaspoons water in a small microwave-safe bowl. Microwave at HIGH 20 seconds or until preserves melt; stir until smooth. Drizzle 1 teaspoon raspberry sauce over each torte; dust each with ½ teaspoon powdered sugar. Yield: 9 servings.

CHOCOLATE-HAZELNUT TORTE

Ground hazelnuts add flavor and bits of crunch to this moist, flourless cake from Capri. Substitute almonds for the hazelnuts, if desired. Or leave out the nuts for a deliciously dark chocolate cake with an incredibly smooth texture with the same **POINTS** value per serving.

Cooking spray
1   tablespoon unsweetened cocoa
3   ounces premium semisweet chocolate, coarsely chopped
¾   cup granulated sugar, divided
½   cup fat-free milk
⅓   cup unsweetened cocoa
2   large eggs
2   large egg whites
⅓   cup ground toasted hazelnuts
½   cup frozen fat-free whipped topping, thawed
1½ teaspoons unsweetened cocoa (optional)
¾   teaspoon powdered sugar (optional)

POINTS value:
4

exchanges:
2 starch
1 fat

per serving:
Calories 191
Fat 6.8g (saturated fat 2.8g)
Protein 5.1g
Carbohydrate 30.3g
Fiber 1.7g
Cholesterol 53mg
Iron 1.3mg
Sodium 41mg
Calcium 36mg

1. Preheat oven to 375°.

2. Coat an 8-inch springform pan with cooking spray, and sprinkle with 1 tablespoon cocoa; set aside.

3. Combine chopped chocolate, ½ cup sugar, milk, and ⅓ cup cocoa in a small saucepan. Cook over low heat 3 minutes or until chocolate melts, stirring constantly with a whisk. Remove from heat. Gradually add hot chocolate mixture to 2 eggs in a bowl, stirring constantly. Return chocolate mixture to pan.

4. Place egg whites in a large bowl; beat with a mixer at high speed until foamy. Gradually add remaining ¼ cup sugar, beating until soft peaks form. Gently fold one-third of egg white mixture into chocolate mixture. Fold in remaining egg white mixture and hazelnuts. Pour into prepared pan. Bake at 375° for 20 minutes or until a wooden pick inserted in center comes out clean. Cool completely in pan on a wire rack. Serve with whipped topping. Dust with cocoa and powdered sugar, if desired. Yield: 8 servings (serving size: 1 torte slice and 1 tablespoon whipped topping).

Note: Grind toasted nuts in a food processor.

PANFORTE
pictured on page 43

Serve this dessert chilled or at room temperature with a cup of coffee or *vinsanto* (Italian sweet wine).

***POINTS* value:**
5

exchanges:
1½ starch
1 fruit
2 fat

per serving:
Calories 249
Fat 9.3g (saturated fat 0.7g)
Protein 4.6g
Carbohydrate 39.5g
Fiber 3.1g
Cholesterol 0mg
Iron 1.6mg
Sodium 4mg
Calcium 52mg

Panforte

(pan-FOHR-tay) is a cross between candy and fruit-cake. This specialty from Siena is a typical Christmas dessert, but it can easily be found year-round in pastry shops throughout Italy.

Cooking spray
⅔ cup all-purpose flour
1 cup whole or slivered almonds, toasted
½ cup whole hazelnuts, toasted
⅓ cup pitted prunes, coarsely chopped
⅓ cup dried Calimyrna figs, coarsely chopped
⅓ cup dried apricots, coarsely chopped
⅓ cup golden raisins
1 teaspoon ground cinnamon
½ teaspoon ground ginger
½ cup honey
⅓ cup granulated sugar
2 tablespoons powdered sugar

1. Preheat oven to 300°.
2. Coat an 8-inch round cake pan with cooking spray. Line bottom with parchment paper; coat with cooking spray.
3. Lightly spoon flour into dry measuring cups, and level with a knife. Combine flour, almonds, and next 7 ingredients in a large bowl; stir until flour coats fruit and nuts. Set aside.
4. Combine honey and granulated sugar in a small saucepan. Cook over low heat until sugar dissolves. Bring syrup to a boil; reduce heat, and simmer, uncovered, 2 minutes. Carefully and quickly add hot syrup to fruit mixture; stir quickly with a wooden spoon to coat. Quickly spread mixture evenly into prepared pan, pressing lightly with back of spoon. Bake at 300° for 30 minutes (mixture will be soft and appear underdone but will firm as it cools). Cool at least 2 hours in pan on a wire rack (or cool 1 day for best results). Remove panforte from pan; remove parchment paper. Sprinkle with powdered sugar. Cut into wedges. Store in refrigerator in an airtight container for up to 1 month. Yield: 12 servings (serving size: 1 wedge).

CITRUS BISCOTTI

¼   cup butter, softened
1   cup sugar
2   large eggs
2   tablespoons frozen orange juice concentrate, thawed
2   tablespoons grated fresh orange rind
1   tablespoon grated fresh lemon rind
1   tablespoon grated fresh lime rind
½   teaspoon vanilla extract
2¾   cups all-purpose flour
1½   teaspoons baking powder
½   teaspoon baking soda
¼   teaspoon salt
Cooking spray
2   teaspoons fresh lemon juice
2   teaspoons sugar

1. Preheat oven to 325°.
2. Beat butter with a mixer at medium speed until creamy. Add 1 cup sugar; beat well. Add eggs, 1 at a time, beating well after each addition. Beat in orange juice concentrate, citrus rinds, and vanilla.
3. Lightly spoon flour into dry measuring cups; level with a knife. Combine flour, baking powder, baking soda, and salt. Gradually add to butter mixture, beating well. Turn dough out onto a lightly floured surface; knead 5 or 6 times. Divide dough in half; shape each half into a 9-inch-long roll. Place rolls, 4 to 5 inches apart, on a baking sheet coated with cooking spray; flatten each roll to 1-inch thickness.
4. Brush dough with lemon juice; sprinkle evenly with 2 teaspoons sugar. Bake at 325° for 29 minutes. Place rolls on a wire rack; cool slightly. While rolls cool, wash any caramelized sugar from baking sheet, and dry thoroughly.
5. Cut rolls diagonally into ½-inch slices. Stand slices upright on baking sheet. Bake at 325° for 17 minutes. Remove cookies from baking sheet, and cool completely on wire rack. Yield: 26 servings (serving size: 1 cookie).

POINTS value:
2

exchanges:
1½ starch

per serving:
Calories 103
Fat 2.3g (saturated fat 1.3g)
Protein 1.9g
Carbohydrate 18.9g
Fiber 0.5g
Cholesterol 21mg
Iron 0.7mg
Sodium 93mg
Calcium 22mg

Biscotti (bee-SKAWT-tee) are so named because they are "twice-baked." These firm, crunchy cookies are perfect for dunking in dessert wine or coffee.

PINE NUT COOKIES

Pine nuts have a light, delicate flavor and are a staple in Italian cuisine. They contribute a buttery quality to these crisp cookies.

POINTS value:
1

exchanges:
½ starch
½ fat

per serving:
Calories 61
Fat 3.5g (saturated fat 0.7g)
Protein 1g
Carbohydrate 6.6g
Fiber 0.2g
Cholesterol 6mg
Iron 0.4mg
Sodium 23mg
Calcium 4mg

¾ cup pine nuts, toasted and divided
1 cup powdered sugar
¼ cup shortening
1 teaspoon vanilla extract
¾ teaspoon almond extract
1 large egg, lightly beaten
1 cup all-purpose flour
¼ teaspoon baking powder
¼ teaspoon salt

1. Place ¼ cup pine nuts in a blender or small food processor; process until ground. Combine ground pine nuts and sugar in a large bowl; cut in shortening with a pastry blender or 2 knives until mixture resembles coarse meal. Add extracts and egg; stir until well blended.
2. Lightly spoon flour into a dry measuring cup; level with a knife. Combine flour, baking powder, and salt; add to shortening mixture. Stir until dough comes together. Cover and chill 30 minutes.
3. Preheat oven to 325°.
4. Shape dough into 35 (¾-inch) balls. Roll balls in ½ cup whole pine nuts; place cookies 2 inches apart on ungreased baking sheets. Bake at 325° for 14 minutes or until lightly browned. Remove from pans; cool completely on wire racks. Yield: 35 servings (serving size: 1 cookie).

SPICED RED WINE AND POMEGRANATE GRANITA

2   cups merlot or other dry red wine
¼   cup sugar
1   (5-inch) cinnamon stick
3   whole cloves
3   (3 x 1–inch) orange rind strips
1   (16-ounce) bottle pomegranate-tangerine juice (such as POM Wonderful)
3½   cups fat-free canned refrigerated whipped topping (such as Reddi-wip)

1. Bring first 5 ingredients to a simmer in a large saucepan over medium heat. Remove from heat; let stand 5 minutes. Strain mixture through a sieve into a bowl; discard solids. Stir juice into wine mixture. Pour mixture into a 13 x 9–inch baking dish. Freeze, uncovered, 1 hour. Scrape entire mixture with a fork to break up ice crystals. Freeze an additional 1 hour, scraping again with a fork after 30 minutes.
2. Scoop ¼ cup granita into each of 7 (10-ounce) stemmed glasses; top each with 2 tablespoons whipped topping. Repeat layers 3 times, ending with whipped topping. Yield: 7 servings.

POINTS value:
2

exchanges:
½ starch
1 fruit

per serving:
Calories 95
Fat 0g (saturated fat 0g)
Protein 0.4g
Carbohydrate 22.7g
Fiber 0g
Cholesterol 0mg
Iron 0.5mg
Sodium 27mg
Calcium 11mg

Granita (grah-nee-TAH), or Italian ice, must be intensely flavorful to be authentic. Creamy whipped topping balances the flavor of the ice.

Granita Tips:
• Although mixtures freeze faster in metal pans, we used a glass dish because this recipe has a high acid content from the wine, and the acid might react with an aluminum pan.
• A fork is the best utensil to scrape the frozen mixture because it produces a nice fine-grain ice.
• Serve the granita in chilled bowls or glasses because the ice melts quickly.

Melon Sorbet

This refreshing sorbet can be served as a light dessert or as a palate cleanser between the starter and main course. Be sure to use ripe, sweet cantaloupe. Purchase the cantaloupe several days in advance, and leave it on your counter to ripen. You'll know it's ripe when you can smell it as you walk into your kitchen. Place the cantaloupe in the refrigerator the day before you plan to make the sorbet so it will be thoroughly chilled.

***POINTS* value:**
2

exchanges:
1 starch
½ fruit

per serving:
Calories 115
Fat 0.1g (saturated fat 0g)
Protein 1.1g
Carbohydrate 24.4g
Fiber 0g
Cholesterol 0mg
Iron 0.2mg
Sodium 41mg
Calcium 8mg

½ cup sweet white wine (such as moscato)
1 (0.3-ounce) package sugar-free peach-flavored gelatin
¾ cup sugar
4 cups cubed ripe cantaloupe (about 1 small), chilled
1 tablespoon fresh lemon juice

1. Combine first 3 ingredients in a small saucepan. Bring to a simmer over medium heat; cook 1 minute. Pour into a metal bowl, and freeze 10 to 12 minutes or until mixture reaches the consistency of egg whites, stirring frequently.
2. Place half of cantaloupe in a blender or food processor; process until puréed and very smooth. Transfer to a large bowl. Repeat with remaining cantaloupe. Stir in wine mixture and lemon juice.
3. Pour mixture into the freezer can of an ice-cream freezer; freeze according to manufacturer's instructions. Yield: 9 servings (serving size: about ½ cup).

AFFOGATO
pictured on page 42

2   cups chocolate low-fat ice cream
¾   cup hot strong brewed coffee
4   teaspoons Grand Marnier (orange-flavored
      liqueur)
¼   cup frozen fat-free whipped topping,
      thawed
1   teaspoon grated fresh orange rind

1. Spoon ½ cup ice cream into each of 4 small bowls or coffee cups; freeze 15 minutes.
2. Pour 3 tablespoons coffee and 1 teaspoon liqueur over each serving. Top each with 1 tablespoon whipped topping and ¼ teaspoon grated orange rind. Serve immediately. Yield: 4 servings.

POINTS value:
3

exchanges:
1½ starch

per serving:
Calories 126
Fat 2g (saturated fat 1g)
Protein 2g
Carbohydrate 21.7g
Fiber 0.1g
Cholesterol 5mg
Iron 0.4mg
Sodium 58mg
Calcium 82mg

Affogato
(ah-foh-GAH-toh),
which means
"drowned," is an
ice cream dessert
that's drowned
in espresso or
strongly brewed
coffee and
alcohol.

LEMON AFFOGATO
pictured on page 42

This refreshing dessert puts a modern twist on the traditional *affogato:* It drowns lemon sorbet in a crisp, cool bath of sparkling water instead of espresso.

POINTS value:
3

exchanges:
1 starch
1½ fruit

per serving:
Calories 145
Fat 0.1g (saturated fat 0g)
Protein 0.1g
Carbohydrate 36.1g
Fiber 0.6g
Cholesterol 0mg
Iron 0.1mg
Sodium 38mg
Calcium 5mg

2   cups lemon sorbet (such as Edy's Whole Fruit Sorbet)
1   cup lemon sparkling water (such as Perrier), chilled
20   fresh raspberries
Mint sprigs (optional)

1. Spoon ½ cup sorbet into each of 4 small bowls or glasses; freeze 15 minutes.

2. Pour ¼ cup sparkling water over each serving; top each with 5 raspberries. Garnish each with a mint sprig, if desired. Serve immediately. Yield: 4 servings.

prep: 12 minutes • **cook:** 10 minutes • **other:** 8 hours and 30 minutes

CAPPUCCINO GELATO

Coffee-flavored Italian ice cream is a treat for the taste buds. One spoonful of this soft-serve treat is all it takes to show you why it's a favorite in Southern Italy.

2½ tablespoons cornstarch
2 tablespoons instant espresso granules or 4 tablespoons instant coffee
2½ cups 2% reduced-fat milk
2 large egg yolks, lightly beaten
1 (14-ounce) can fat-free sweetened condensed milk
¾ cup fat-free half-and-half
2 teaspoons vanilla extract
¼ teaspoon ground cinnamon (optional)
⅛ teaspoon salt

POINTS value:
5

exchanges:
2½ starch

per serving:
Calories 219
Fat 2.9g (saturated fat 1.5g)
Protein 7.7g
Carbohydrate 39.1g
Fiber 0g
Cholesterol 64mg
Iron 0.2mg
Sodium 161mg
Calcium 248mg

> **_Gelato_** (jeh-LAH-toh) is the Italian word for "ice cream."

1. Combine cornstarch and espresso granules in a large saucepan; gradually add milk, stirring with a whisk until well blended. Bring to a boil over medium heat, and cook 1 minute or until slightly thick, stirring constantly. Remove from heat. Gradually whisk about one-fourth of hot coffee mixture into egg yolks, and add to remaining hot coffee mixture, whisking constantly. Cook over medium-low heat 2 minutes or until a thermometer reaches 160°, stirring constantly. Remove from heat.

2. Pour coffee mixture into a bowl; stir in sweetened condensed milk and remaining ingredients. Cover and chill 8 hours or overnight.

3. Pour mixture into the freezer can of 4-quart ice-cream freezer, and freeze according to manufacturer's instructions. Yield: 8 servings (serving size: ½ cup).

LEMON SEMIFREDDO

This refreshing lemon version of semifreddo was a hit with our taste-testing panel. It's ideal for entertaining because of the large yield. Garnish each serving with fresh mint leaves and a few fresh berries to make it extraspecial.

POINTS value:
3

exchanges:
2½ starch

per serving:
Calories 166
Fat 0.1g (saturated fat 0.1g)
Protein 3.8g
Carbohydrate 36.5g
Fiber 0.1g
Cholesterol 1mg
Iron 0.1mg
Sodium 63mg
Calcium 132mg

> **Semifreddo**
> *(say-mee-FRAYD-doh) is an Italian whipped cream that is served half-frozen so that it has a rich and creamy texture. It can be flavored with anything from vanilla to coffee.*

3   cups vanilla fat-free yogurt
¾   cup sugar
2   teaspoons grated fresh lemon rind
½   cup fresh lemon juice
1   (8-ounce) container frozen fat-free whipped topping, thawed

1. Line an 8½ x 4½–inch loaf pan with plastic wrap, allowing plastic wrap to extend over edges of pan; set aside.
2. Combine first 4 ingredients in a large bowl; stir well. Gently fold in whipped topping. Spoon into prepared pan, and freeze at least 8 hours or until firm. Let stand at room temperature 10 minutes; unmold and remove plastic wrap. Cut into slices. Yield: 14 servings (serving size: 1 slice).

Note: For individual servings, place 14 jumbo aluminum muffin liners on a baking sheet. Spoon ½ cup semifreddo mixture into each liner. Freeze 3 hours or until firm. Store in an airtight container in freezer up to 1 month.

Entrées

SEA BASS AL CARTOCCIO

The packets can be prepped up to 24 hours ahead, refrigerated, and then baked for a no-fuss dinner on busy evenings. Be sure to enjoy the delicious cooking broth over rice or noodles, or serve bread to soak up the juices.

POINTS value:
6

exchanges:
1 vegetable
4 lean meat

per serving:
Calories 245
Fat 10.6g (saturated fat 1.8g)
Protein 31.9g
Carbohydrate 3.5g
Fiber 0.9g
Cholesterol 70mg
Iron 0.7mg
Sodium 409mg
Calcium 35mg

Al cartoccio
(ahl kahr-TOH-chee-oh) literally means "in a bag," and these neat little packets are a handy, delicious way to cook fish.

1	tablespoon chopped fresh oregano
2	tablespoons olive oil, divided
2	teaspoons chopped fresh thyme
2	teaspoons minced garlic
¾	teaspoon freshly ground black pepper
½	teaspoon salt
4	(6-ounce) sea bass or halibut fillets (about 1 inch thick)
8	(¼-inch-thick) slices lemon (about 2 lemons)
2	plum tomatoes, each cut into 6 wedges

1. Preheat oven to 400°.

2. Cut 4 (12-inch) squares of parchment paper or heavy-duty foil; spread squares out on work surface.

3. Combine oregano, 1 tablespoon oil, and next 4 ingredients in a small bowl; rub evenly over all sides of fish. Place 1 piece of fish in center of each parchment square; top each piece of fish with 2 lemon slices and 3 tomato wedges. Drizzle remaining 1 tablespoon oil evenly over fish fillets; seal the packets closed so they are airtight. Place packets on a jelly-roll pan or in a baking pan with sides.

4. Bake at 400° for 25 minutes or until fish flakes easily when tested with a fork (remove 1 packet and check for doneness before removing the others from the oven). Place packets on individual plates; cut open top of each packet with a knife. Serve immediately. Yield: 4 servings.

Simple Parchment Packets: Parchment-paper packets seal in the juices and flavors while steaming the fish, resulting in a mess-free, mouthwatering entrée. While parchment paper is traditional, aluminum foil works just as well, and it's standard in every kitchen. If using parchment paper, one way to seal the packet is to make the candy-shaped fold.

1. Fold the paper over the fish like a book, and then seal the long edge with narrow folds.

2. Gather the paper at the ends, and tie with kitchen twine.

Tuna Steaks with Basil Gremolata

Gremolata typically accompanies osso buco (braised veal shanks). However, with no fat to speak of, it's a flavor boost you can feel good about using anywhere you fancy. Here, basil shares the stage with the usual parsley, and the result is a perfect pairing for tuna. You can grill or broil the tuna steaks, but we preferred the flavor and appearance of the grilled fish.

POINTS value:
6

exchanges:
½ starch
7 very lean meat

per serving:
Calories 288
Fat 4.7g (saturated fat 0.9g)
Protein 52.2g
Carbohydrate 6g
Fiber 0.8g
Cholesterol 99mg
Iron 2.3mg
Sodium 349mg
Calcium 62mg

> **Gremolata**
> (greh-moh-LAH-tah) is a savory relish of lemon rind, garlic, and fresh herbs.

⅓ cup chopped fresh basil
2 tablespoons chopped fresh flat-leaf parsley
1 tablespoon grated fresh lemon rind
⅛ teaspoon salt
⅛ teaspoon black pepper
2 garlic cloves, minced
4 (6-ounce) tuna steaks (about 1 inch thick)
2 teaspoons olive oil
¼ teaspoon salt
¼ teaspoon black pepper
½ cup dry breadcrumbs
Cooking spray

1. Combine first 6 ingredients in a small bowl; set aside.
2. Prepare grill or preheat broiler.
3. Rub each tuna steak evenly with olive oil; sprinkle tuna with ¼ teaspoon salt and ¼ teaspoon pepper. Dredge tuna in breadcrumbs, shaking off excess.
4. Place tuna on grill rack or broiler pan coated with cooking spray; cook 3 minutes on each side or until fish is medium-rare or desired degree of doneness. Place tuna steaks on individual plates, and top with gremolata. Yield: 4 servings (serving size: 1 tuna steak and about 2 tablespoons gremolata).

SHRIMP FRA DIAVOLO

Reduce the crushed red pepper in this recipe if you prefer a less spicy entrée. Spicy or not, the fragrance of fire-roasted tomatoes, rosemary, and garlic fills the kitchen with a mouthwatering aroma. You can substitute fat-free, less-sodium chicken broth for the wine, but our tasting panel preferred the wine-flavored version. Serve this dish with a fresh garden salad and a glass of your favorite wine.

1	(9-ounce) package refrigerated fresh fettuccine
1½	pounds large shrimp, peeled and deveined
1	tablespoon olive oil, divided
¾	teaspoon crushed red pepper, divided
1	tablespoon finely chopped fresh rosemary
3	tablespoons minced garlic (about 12 cloves)
½	cup dry white wine
½	cup bottled clam juice
¼	teaspoon salt
1	(28-ounce) can fire-roasted diced tomatoes, undrained
¼	cup chopped fresh flat-leaf parsley

1. Cook pasta in a Dutch oven according to package directions, omitting salt and fat.

2. While water comes to a boil and pasta cooks, combine shrimp, 1½ teaspoons olive oil, and ½ teaspoon crushed red pepper in a bowl; toss well to coat shrimp. Heat a large nonstick skillet over medium-high heat 2 minutes or until very hot. Add shrimp; sauté 1 minute. Remove shrimp from pan; set aside. Reduce heat to medium.

3. Add remaining 1½ teaspoons oil, rosemary, and garlic to pan; sauté 3 minutes or until fragrant. Add wine and clam juice; bring to a boil over medium-high heat. Boil 5 minutes or until liquid is reduced by half. Add remaining ¼ teaspoon crushed red pepper, salt, and tomatoes; return to a boil over medium-high heat, and cook 5 minutes, stirring frequently. Stir in shrimp and any juices; remove from heat.

4. Drain pasta well, and return to Dutch oven. Add shrimp mixture and parsley; toss well. Serve immediately. Yield: 5 servings (serving size: about 1½ cups).

POINTS value:
7

exchanges:
2 starch
2 vegetable
3 very lean meat
1 fat

per serving:
Calories 357
Fat 5.9g (saturated fat 0.7g)
Protein 29.1g
Carbohydrate 39.5g
Fiber 4.3g
Cholesterol 202mg
Iron 5.6mg
Sodium 756mg
Calcium 107mg

Fra diavolo (frah de-AH-voh-loh), which translates as "brother devil," is a term that refers to a spicy dish that's seasoned heavily with black or red pepper.

SEAFOOD RISOTTO MILANESE

Italy and pasta pretty much go hand in hand, but in northern Italy, rice is the starch of choice. Risotto is made with Arborio rice (a short-grained Italian rice), and it's traditionally cooked on the stovetop. The rice is briefly fried in oil before the broth is added in stages. Constant stirring results in an ultracreamy dish. We shortened the cook time and the amount of stirring by using the microwave. The addition of shrimp and scallops makes for an outstanding entrée.

POINTS value:
5

exchanges:
1½ starch
1 vegetable
2 lean meat

per serving:
Calories 236
Fat 5.8g (saturated fat 2.3g)
Protein 19.4g
Carbohydrate 25.6g
Fiber 1.1g
Cholesterol 78mg
Iron 1.7mg
Sodium 632mg
Calcium 56mg

In Milan, saffron is added to risotto to create **risotto Milanese** *(rih-SAW-toh mee-lah-NAY-zay), which is typically served as a side to osso buco.*

5   cups fat-free, less-sodium chicken broth, divided
½   teaspoon saffron threads
2   teaspoons olive oil
1½   cups sliced cremini or button mushrooms
1   cup chopped onion (about 1 small)
2   teaspoons minced garlic
1½   cups uncooked Arborio rice
1   cup dry white wine or fat-free, less-sodium chicken broth
¼   teaspoon crushed red pepper
¼   teaspoon ground black pepper
1   cup chopped seeded plum tomato (2 tomatoes)
½   pound medium shrimp, peeled and deveined
½   pound sea scallops, cut in half horizontally
3   tablespoons chopped fresh flat-leaf parsley
1½   tablespoons butter
1   tablespoon grated fresh Parmesan cheese

1. Place ½ cup chicken broth and saffron threads in a small microwave-safe bowl; microwave at HIGH 1 minute. Remove from microwave; set aside.

2. Place oil in a large glass microwave-safe bowl, and microwave at HIGH 1 minute. Add mushrooms, onion, and garlic; stir well. Cover with plastic wrap, and vent; microwave at HIGH 1 minute.

3. Stir in rice. Cover and microwave at HIGH 4 minutes. Strain saffron mixture; discard threads. Stir in saffron broth, remaining 4½ cups chicken broth, wine, and peppers; microwave, uncovered, at HIGH 16 minutes, stirring after 9 minutes.

4. Stir in tomato, shrimp, and scallops; microwave, uncovered, at HIGH 2 minutes or until shrimp turn pink and scallops are done. Stir in parsley and butter. Let stand 5 minutes. Spoon into individual bowls; sprinkle with cheese. Yield: 6 servings (serving size: about 1 cup risotto and ½ teaspoon cheese).

Quick Tips: To keep preparation time to a minimum, check out these tips from our Test Kitchens.

1. Purchase prechopped onion and tomato, preminced garlic, and presliced mushrooms in the produce department of large supermarkets.

2. Look for peeled and deveined shrimp in the seafood department. As a rule of thumb, 1 pound of shrimp in the shell equals ¾ pound of peeled, deveined shrimp. For the half pound of shrimp in the shell called for in this recipe, you'll need about 6½ ounces of peeled, deveined shrimp.

3. Place the parsley in a glass measuring cup, and chop quickly with kitchen shears.

SHRIMP SCAMPI ON COUSCOUS

Couscous, although typically thought of as an African dish, belongs to Sicilian tradition, too, and is almost always served with the seafood that is so bountiful in that area.

POINTS value:
8

exchanges:
2 starch
2 vegetable
4 very lean meat
1 fat

per serving:
Calories 401
Fat 7.9g (saturated fat 1.2g)
Protein 37.2g
Carbohydrate 44.2g
Fiber 5.3g
Cholesterol 280mg
Iron 6.1mg
Sodium 967mg
Calcium 124mg

1   cup water
⅔   cup uncooked couscous
2   teaspoons olive oil
¾   cup chopped onion
4   garlic cloves, minced
1¼   pounds large shrimp, peeled and deveined
1   (14.5-ounce) can petite diced tomatoes, undrained
¼   cup coarsely chopped pitted kalamata olives
¼   cup dry white wine or fat-free, less-sodium chicken broth
1   tablespoon capers
½   teaspoon grated fresh lemon rind
1   tablespoon fresh lemon juice
¼   teaspoon salt
¼   teaspoon freshly ground black pepper
¼   cup chopped fresh flat-leaf parsley
¼   cup chopped fresh basil

1. Bring 1 cup water to a boil in a medium saucepan; stir in couscous. Remove from heat; cover and let stand 5 minutes or until water is absorbed. Fluff with a fork; keep warm.
2. While water boils and couscous stands, heat oil in a large nonstick skillet over medium-high heat. Add onion and garlic; sauté 3 minutes or until tender. Add shrimp; sauté 2 minutes or until just done. Add tomatoes and next 7 ingredients. Bring to a boil; reduce heat, and simmer, uncovered, 2 minutes. Remove from heat; stir in parsley and basil. Serve over couscous. Yield: 3 servings (serving size: 1 cup shrimp mixture and ⅔ cup couscous).

Note: To prepare couscous in the microwave, add 1 cup water to a 2- or 4-cup glass measure. Microwave at HIGH 1 to 2 minutes or until boiling; stir in couscous. Cover with plastic wrap, and let stand 5 minutes or until water is absorbed. Fluff with a fork.

MUSHROOM RAGÙ WITH POLENTA
pictured on page 78

To speed things up, this recipe is served over prepared refrigerated polenta slices. If you prefer to make your own polenta, try Herbed Polenta with Parmigiano-Reggiano on page 152 or use instant polenta. There's no need to shape and pan-fry it; just serve it in a bowl straight from the saucepan and top it with the ragù. The ragù makes a delicious topping for pasta, too.

1	tablespoon olive oil
½	cup diced celery (about 1 stalk)
½	cup chopped red onion (about ½ small)
⅓	cup diced carrot (about 4 medium)
1	tablespoon minced garlic
2	(8-ounce) packages sliced baby portobello mushrooms
1	(28-ounce) can diced tomatoes with basil, garlic, and oregano, drained
1	tablespoon grated fresh lemon rind
¼	teaspoon crushed red pepper
1	(17-ounce) package prepared refrigerated basil and garlic–flavored polenta, cut into 12 slices (such as Marjon)

Cooking spray

2	tablespoons grated Parmesan cheese

POINTS value:
5

exchanges:
1½ starch
4 vegetable
½ fat

per serving:
Calories 246
Fat 4.8g (saturated fat 0.9g)
Protein 8.1g
Carbohydrate 42.9g
Fiber 4.7g
Cholesterol 2mg
Iron 3.6mg
Sodium 1,194mg
Calcium 156mg

1. Heat oil in a large nonstick skillet over medium heat. Add celery and next 3 ingredients; sauté 3 minutes or until vegetables are crisp-tender. Add mushrooms, and sauté 8 minutes or until mushrooms release their liquid. Stir in tomatoes, lemon rind, and red pepper. Increase heat to medium–high, and cook 3 minutes. Remove ragù from pan; wipe pan clean with paper towels. Keep ragù warm.
2. Place pan over medium-high heat. Coat polenta slices with cooking spray; add to pan. Cook 4 to 5 minutes on each side or until browned.
3. Serve mushroom ragù over polenta in individual bowls; sprinkle with cheese. Yield: 4 servings (serving size: 3 polenta slices, 1 cup ragù, and 1½ teaspoons cheese).

EGGPLANT PARMESAN

Adding a few simple ingredients to commercial marinara sauce makes it taste more authentic. Fat-free mayonnaise is the secret ingredient to getting the breadcrumbs to stick to the eggplant.

POINTS **value:**
5

exchanges:
1 starch
3 vegetable
1 high-fat meat

per serving:
Calories 266
Fat 10.2g (saturated fat 4.2g)
Protein 13g
Carbohydrate 29.3g
Fiber 7.5g
Cholesterol 24mg
Iron 1.6mg
Sodium 968mg
Calcium 315mg

1   (26-ounce) jar marinara sauce (such as Bertolli)
2   tablespoons balsamic vinegar
½   teaspoon crushed red pepper
¼   teaspoon black pepper
¾   cup dry breadcrumbs
½   cup grated Parmesan cheese
1   teaspoon dried Italian seasoning
¼   teaspoon salt
¼   teaspoon ground black pepper
⅓   cup fat-free mayonnaise
1   (1½-pound) eggplant, peeled and cut into ¼-inch-thick slices
Cooking spray
1½ cups (6 ounces) shredded part-skim mozzarella cheese, divided

1. Preheat oven to 425°.

2. Combine first 4 ingredients; stir well. Set aside.

3. Combine breadcrumbs and next 4 ingredients in a pie plate or shallow dish; stir well. Spread mayonnaise over both sides of eggplant slices, and dredge in breadcrumb mixture. Set aside ¼ cup leftover breadcrumb mixture. Place eggplant slices on a baking sheet coated with cooking spray. Bake at 425° for 16 minutes or until lightly browned. Remove eggplant from oven. Reduce oven temperature to 375°.

4. Spoon ½ cup marinara sauce mixture in bottom of an 11 x 7–inch baking dish coated with cooking spray. Arrange half of eggplant slices over sauce. Pour about 1 cup marinara sauce over eggplant slices, and sprinkle with ¾ cup mozzarella cheese. Repeat procedure with remaining eggplant, marinara sauce, and cheese; top with reserved ¼ cup breadcrumb mixture.

5. Bake, uncovered, at 375° for 20 minutes or until bubbly. Let stand 5 minutes before serving. Yield: 6 servings.

Grilled Veal Chops with Artichoke-Arugula Salad, page 86

Mushroom Ragù with
Polenta, page 75

Pizza Quattro
Stagioni, page 92

Prosciutto, Mozzarella, and
Arugula Panini, page 91

BEEF BRACIOLA

We updated this popular dish from southern Italy by using a slow cooker
so that you don't have to tend to it while it cooks.

1	(1¼-pound) flank steak, trimmed
1½	cups Caesar salad–flavored restaurant-style croutons
⅓	cup grated Parmesan cheese
1½	teaspoons minced garlic
6	sprigs each of parsley, oregano, and thyme
3	large egg whites
½	teaspoon black pepper
Cooking spray	
1	(26-ounce) jar marinara sauce (such as Newman's Own)

1. Place steak between 2 sheets of heavy-duty plastic wrap;
flatten to ¼-inch thickness using a meat mallet or rolling pin.
2. Place croutons and next 4 ingredients in a food processor or blender; process until mixture forms a paste. Spread
mixture evenly over steak to within ½ inch of edges. Roll
up steak, beginning with a narrow end, and tie with
kitchen twine. Sprinkle evenly with pepper.
3. Heat a large nonstick skillet over medium-high heat;
coat pan with cooking spray. Add steak roll, and cook 8
minutes or until browned, turning occasionally.
4. Pour sauce into a 3-quart electric slow cooker; top with
steak roll. Cover and cook on HIGH 1 hour. Reduce heat
to LOW; cook 5 hours or until steak is tender. Cut braciola
into 10 slices. Serve with marinara sauce. Yield: 5 servings
(serving size: 2 braciola slices and ⅔ cup sauce).

POINTS value:
8

exchanges:
½ starch
3 vegetable
4 lean meat

per serving:
Calories 350
Fat 13.5g (saturated fat 3.4g)
Protein 33.9g
Carbohydrate 21.6g
Fiber 0.1g
Cholesterol 43mg
Iron 1.9mg
Sodium 942mg
Calcium 136mg

Beef braciola
(brah-chee-OH-
lah) refers to a
cut of meat, usu-
ally flank steak,
that is topped
with bread-
crumbs, cheese,
and herbs before
it is rolled up and
slowly baked.

STEAK FLORENTINE

This satisfying beef dish hails from Florence. Traditionally, a thick-cut T-bone is the meat of choice, but we've substituted filet mignon to significantly cut the fat. A paste of fresh garlic, rosemary, and olive oil infuses the steaks with flavor.

POINTS value:
5

exchanges:
3 lean meat

per serving:
Calories 184
Fat 10.9g (saturated fat 3.3g)
Protein 18.4g
Carbohydrate 2.2g
Fiber 0.3g
Cholesterol 54mg
Iron 2.7mg
Sodium 278mg
Calcium 32mg

1	tablespoon olive oil
2½	teaspoons chopped fresh rosemary
4	garlic cloves, peeled
½	teaspoon kosher salt or ¼ teaspoon table salt
½	teaspoon freshly ground black pepper
4	(4-ounce) beef tenderloin steaks (1½ inches thick), trimmed

Cooking spray

2	cups trimmed arugula or spinach
4	lemon wedges

1. Prepare grill.
2. Place first 3 ingredients in a blender; process until mixture forms a paste, stopping blender and scraping down sides frequently.
3. Sprinkle salt and pepper evenly over both sides of steaks; spread garlic paste evenly over both sides of steaks.
4. Place steaks on grill rack coated with cooking spray, and grill 5 minutes on each side or until desired degree of doneness.
5. Place ½ cup arugula on each of 4 plates; top each with 1 steak. Squeeze a lemon wedge over each serving. Yield: 4 servings.

prep: 18 minutes • **cook:** 1 hour and 50 minutes

OSSO BUCO WITH GREMOLATA

Both cooking methods given here (stovetop and slow cooker) yield moist, tender meat with a hearty sauce—perfect for serving over soft polenta or mashed potatoes.

4	(8- to 9-ounce) veal shanks
½	teaspoon salt, divided
1	teaspoon freshly ground black pepper
¼	cup all-purpose flour
2	tablespoons olive oil, divided
2	cups baby carrots
1	cup chopped onion
1	cup chopped celery
3	garlic cloves, minced
⅓	cup Marsala wine
1	(14-ounce) can fat-free, less-sodium beef broth
¼	cup finely chopped fresh flat-leaf parsley
1	teaspoon grated fresh lemon rind
2	garlic cloves, minced

POINTS value:
6

exchanges:
3 vegetable
4 lean meat

per serving:
Calories 298
Fat 10.9g (saturated fat 2g)
Protein 31.4g
Carbohydrate 17.5g
Fiber 3g
Cholesterol 112mg
Iron 2.7mg
Sodium 649mg
Calcium 94mg

> **Osso Buco**
> (AW-soh BOO-koh), or braised veal shanks, is the ultimate in rustic Italian cooking.

1. Sprinkle veal shanks evenly with ¼ teaspoon salt and pepper; dredge in flour, shaking off excess.
2. Heat 1 tablespoon oil in a Dutch oven over medium-high heat. Add veal shanks, and cook 5 minutes on each side or until browned. Remove veal from pan. Heat remaining 1 tablespoon oil in pan over medium-high heat. Add carrots, onion, celery, and 3 garlic cloves; sauté 6 minutes. Add remaining ¼ teaspoon salt, Marsala, and broth; bring to a boil. Return veal to pan. Reduce heat, cover, and simmer 1 hour. Uncover and simmer 30 minutes.
3. While veal is simmering, combine parsley, lemon rind, and 2 garlic cloves. Place 1 veal shank in each of 4 shallow bowls; spoon about ¾ cup sauce over each serving, and sprinkle each with 1 tablespoon gremolata. Yield: 4 servings.

> **Slow-Cooker Method:** Place browned shanks in a 5-quart electric slow cooker; top with sautéed vegetables. Add remaining ¼ teaspoon salt, Marsala, and broth. Cover with lid; cook on HIGH 1 hour. Reduce heat to LOW; cook 5 hours. Serve with gremolata.

prep: 19 minutes • **cook:** 17 minutes

VEAL MARSALA

Sweet Marsala wine from Sicily adds a signature rich, smoky flavor to this classic dish. Look for very thin scallops (slices) of boneless veal, sometimes labeled as veal scaloppine; these are the most tender. If the thinner scallops are not available, place thicker veal cutlets in a large heavy-duty zip-top plastic bag or between two sheets of heavy-duty plastic wrap, and flatten to a ⅛-inch thickness using a meat mallet or rolling pin. Also try this recipe with chicken breasts or pork cutlets.

POINTS value:
7

exchanges:
½ starch
1 vegetable
3 medium-fat meat

per serving:
Calories 299
Fat 16.5g (saturated fat 7.8g)
Protein 21.1g
Carbohydrate 11.2g
Fiber 0.7g
Cholesterol 89mg
Iron 1.7mg
Sodium 355mg
Calcium 29mg

1	(3.5-ounce) package fresh shiitake mushrooms
1	pound very thin veal cutlets (about 8 pieces; ⅛ inch thick)
½	teaspoon freshly ground black pepper
¼	teaspoon salt
¼	cup all-purpose flour
2	tablespoons butter, divided
¼	cup minced shallot (about 1 large)
2	garlic cloves, minced
1	cup fat-free, less-sodium beef broth
½	cup sweet Marsala wine
1	tablespoon fresh lemon juice
2	tablespoons chopped fresh flat-leaf parsley

1. Remove and discard stems from shiitake mushrooms. Slice mushroom caps; set aside.

2. Sprinkle veal with pepper and salt; lightly dredge in flour, shaking off excess.

3. Heat 2 teaspoons butter in a large nonstick skillet over medium-high heat until butter begins to foam. Add half of veal; cook 30 seconds to 1 minute on each side or until lightly browned. Remove veal from pan; keep warm. Repeat procedure with 2 teaspoons butter and remaining veal.

4. Melt remaining 2 teaspoons butter in pan over medium-high heat. Add sliced mushrooms, shallot, and garlic; sauté 2 minutes. Add broth and Marsala, scraping pan to loosen browned bits. Bring to a boil, and cook 5 minutes or until liquid is reduced to 1 cup. Return veal and any juices to pan. Stir in lemon juice; bring to a boil. Remove from heat, and sprinkle with parsley. Yield: 4 servings (serving size: 3 ounces veal and ¼ cup sauce).

VEAL PICCATA

Cooking the veal in batches ensures that the meat browns nicely. Chicken or pork cutlets may be substituted for veal.

¼   cup all-purpose flour
¾   teaspoon salt, divided
¼   teaspoon ground white pepper
1   pound very thin veal cutlets (about 8 pieces)
1   tablespoon olive oil, divided
1   cup fat-free, less-sodium chicken broth
2   tablespoons fresh lemon juice
1   tablespoon butter
1   tablespoon chopped fresh flat-leaf parsley
1   tablespoon capers

1. Combine flour, ½ teaspoon salt, and pepper in a shallow dish. Dredge veal in flour mixture, shaking off excess.
2. Heat 1½ teaspoons oil in a large nonstick skillet over medium-high heat. Add half of veal, and cook 1 minute on each side or until lightly browned. Remove veal from pan, and keep warm. Repeat procedure with remaining 1½ teaspoons oil and remaining veal.
3. Add chicken broth and lemon juice to pan; cook 4 minutes or until liquid is reduced to about ¼ cup, scraping pan to loosen browned bits. Whisk in butter and remaining ¼ teaspoon salt; remove from heat. Spoon sauce over veal; sprinkle with parsley and capers. Yield: 4 servings (serving size: 3 ounces veal, 1 tablespoon sauce, ¾ teaspoon parsley, and ¾ teaspoon capers).

POINTS **value:**
7

exchanges:
½ starch
3 medium-fat meat

per serving:
Calories 260
Fat 17g (saturated fat 6.5g)
Protein 20.3g
Carbohydrate 5.6g
Fiber 0.3g
Cholesterol 81mg
Iron 1.1mg
Sodium 713mg
Calcium 22mg

Tart lemon juice, briny capers, and fresh parsley complement veal's delicate flavor in **veal piccata** *(pih-KAH-tuh), a popular Italian dish.*

GRILLED VEAL CHOPS WITH ARTICHOKE–ARUGULA SALAD
pictured on page 77

Italians have a love for bitter greens such as arugula, which grows wild in Italy. The intense peppery-mustard flavor of arugula works nicely with these simple grilled veal chops, creating a meal worthy of company with minimal effort. Prepare the veal chops up to four hours ahead, and grill them just before you're ready to eat.

POINTS value:
8

exchanges:
2 vegetable
3 medium-fat meat
1½ fat

per serving:
Calories 356
Fat 22.2g (saturated fat 6.1g)
Protein 28.3g
Carbohydrate 10.2g
Fiber 3.4g
Cholesterol 100mg
Iron 1.7mg
Sodium 774mg
Calcium 87mg

4   (7–ounce) veal loin chops (about ½ inch thick)
¾   teaspoon freshly ground black pepper, divided
½   teaspoon salt, divided
1½ tablespoons olive oil, divided
1   teaspoon grated fresh lemon rind
3   garlic cloves, minced
Cooking Spray
1   (5–ounce) package baby arugula or spinach
1   (14–ounce) can artichoke bottoms, drained and thinly sliced
¼   cup coarsely chopped walnuts, toasted
1   tablespoon fresh lemon juice

1. Sprinkle veal chops evenly with ½ teaspoon pepper and ¼ teaspoon salt. Combine 1½ teaspoons olive oil, lemon rind, and garlic; rub over veal chops. Cover and chill 1 to 4 hours.
2. Prepare grill.
3. Place veal chops on grill rack coated with cooking spray; grill 4 minutes on each side or until desired degree of doneness.
4. While veal grills, combine arugula, artichokes, and walnuts in a bowl. Combine remaining ¼ teaspoon each of pepper and salt, remaining 1 tablespoon olive oil, and lemon juice; drizzle over salad, and toss well. Serve immediately with veal chops. Yield: 4 servings (serving size: 1 veal chop and 2 cups salad).

ROSEMARY LAMB CHOPS WITH GARLIC-BALSAMIC SAUCE

It's traditional in Rome to serve lamb for Easter, but these chops are too tasty and easy to wait for a holiday. From start to finish, they're ready in less than 30 minutes, making them ideal for busy weeknights. Add some steamed broccoli and rice, and dinner is ready.

1   tablespoon minced garlic, divided
½   teaspoon salt, divided
2   tablespoons chopped fresh rosemary
2   tablespoons stone-ground mustard
1   tablespoon olive oil
2   teaspoons balsamic vinegar
8   (4-ounce) lamb loin chops, trimmed
½   cup balsamic vinegar
½   teaspoon black pepper

1. Prepare grill.
2. Combine 1 teaspoon garlic, ¼ teaspoon salt, rosemary, mustard, olive oil, and 2 teaspoons vinegar in a small bowl; stir well.
3. Place lamb chops in a shallow dish. Spread rosemary mixture evenly over both sides of chops; let stand at room temperature 10 minutes.
4. While chops stand, bring ½ cup balsamic vinegar and remaining 2 teaspoons garlic to a boil in a small saucepan. Reduce heat, and simmer, uncovered, 5 minutes or until reduced to ¼ cup. Stir in remaining ¼ teaspoon salt and pepper; set aside, and keep warm.
5. Place lamb chops on grill rack; cover and grill 4 minutes on each side or until desired degree of doneness. Place lamb chops on each of 4 plates, and drizzle with vinegar mixture. Yield: 4 servings (serving size: 2 lamb chops and 1 tablespoon sauce).

POINTS **value:**
7

exchanges:
½ starch
4 lean meat

per serving:
Calories 272
Fat 13.2g (saturated fat 3.8g)
Protein 28.6g
Carbohydrate 5.7g
Fiber 0.1g
Cholesterol 90mg
Iron 2.3mg
Sodium 480mg
Calcium 31mg

Pork Milanese

The simple preparation this dish requires is truly hard to beat. Rather than pan-frying, we opted to "oven-fry," which reduced the amount of fat in the recipe. We used pork chops, but it's also delicious made with chicken breasts or veal cutlets.

POINTS value:
5

exchanges:
½ starch
4 very lean meat
1 fat

per serving:
Calories 231
Fat 9.3g (saturated fat 3.5g)
Protein 27.5g
Carbohydrate 8.5g
Fiber 1.3g
Cholesterol 97mg
Iron 1.6mg
Sodium 358mg
Calcium 87mg

> **Pork Milanese**
> (mee-lah-NAY-zay), a traditional dish from Milan, is simply a piece of meat that is dipped in egg, dredged in breadcrumbs and Parmesan cheese, and then pan-fried and doused with lemon juice.

4   (4-ounce) boneless center-cut pork chops, trimmed
2   (1.2-ounce) slices whole wheat bread
¼   cup grated fresh Parmigiano-Reggiano cheese
1   teaspoon dried Italian seasoning
2   teaspoons olive oil
¼   teaspoon salt
⅛   teaspoon freshly ground black pepper
1   garlic clove, minced
1   tablespoon water
1   large egg
Cooking spray
4   lemon wedges

1. Preheat oven to 450°.
2. Place pork chops between 2 sheets of heavy-duty plastic wrap, and flatten to ¼-inch thickness using a meat mallet or rolling pin. Set aside.
3. Place bread in a food processor, and pulse 10 times to form coarse crumbs that measure 1½ cups. Place bread-crumbs in a pie plate or shallow dish. Stir in cheese and next 5 ingredients.
4. Combine water and egg in a bowl; stir well with a whisk. Dip pork chops in egg mixture; dredge in bread-crumb mixture.
5. Place pork chops on a baking sheet coated with cook-ing spray. Bake at 450° for 20 minutes or until done. Squeeze a lemon wedge over each chop. Yield: 4 servings (serving size: 1 chop).

ARISTA

2 cups water
6 garlic cloves
1½ teaspoons chopped fresh rosemary
2 teaspoons olive oil
½ teaspoon salt
⅛ teaspoon freshly ground black pepper
2 (¾-pound) pork tenderloins, trimmed
Cooking spray
1 cup fat-free, less-sodium chicken broth
½ cup dry white wine
⅛ teaspoon salt

1. Preheat oven to 425°.
2. Bring 2 cups water to a simmer in a small saucepan. Add garlic; simmer 1 minute. Drain well; finely chop garlic. Combine garlic, rosemary, and next 3 ingredients in a small bowl; mash with a fork to form a paste.
3. Slice each tenderloin lengthwise, cutting to, but not through, other side. Open halves, laying pork flat. Cut each side lengthwise, cutting to, not through, other side; open flat. Place heavy-duty plastic wrap over pork, and flatten to ½-inch thickness using a meat mallet or rolling pin.
4. Set aside 2 teaspoons rosemary-garlic paste. Rub remaining paste onto cut sides of pork. Roll up each tenderloin; secure at 2-inch intervals with kitchen twine. Rub outside of pork with reserved 2 teaspoons paste.
5. Heat a large nonstick skillet over medium-high heat; coat pan with cooking spray. Add tenderloins; cook 5 minutes, browning on all sides. Place tenderloins on a broiler pan coated with cooking spray. Bake at 425° for 20 minutes or until a thermometer registers 155° (slightly pink). Let stand 10 minutes.
6. While pork stands, add broth and wine to skillet. Bring to a simmer; cook 5 minutes or until reduced to ½ cup. Remove from heat; stir in ⅛ teaspoon salt. Cut pork into thin slices; serve with wine mixture. Yield: 6 servings (serving size: 3 ounces pork and about 1 tablespoon sauce).

POINTS value:
4

exchanges:
3 lean meat

per serving:
Calories 158
Fat 5.4g (saturated fat 1.5g)
Protein 24.5g
Carbohydrate 1.5g
Fiber 0.1g
Cholesterol 74mg
Iron 1.6mg
Sodium 396mg
Calcium 15mg

In Tuscany, **arista** (ah-rist-TAH), or pork roast, is usually spit- or oven-roasted and seasoned with rosemary, salt, and pepper. Tuscans prefer to eat the meat cold. Here, it's served warm with a wine sauce, but chilled leftovers can be thinly sliced for tasty panini (Italian sandwiches).

GNOCCHI WITH PUMPKIN AND SAGE
pictured on page 2

Pumpkin gnocchi with sage butter is common on Italian tables. We started with ready-made potato gnocchi and made a lusciously creamy pumpkin sauce that's seasoned with sage and crispy pancetta.

POINTS value:
7

exchanges:
3 starch
1½ vegetable
1 fat

per serving:
Calories 324
Fat 8.9g (saturated fat 3.3g)
Protein 9.3g
Carbohydrate 53.6g
Fiber 3.6g
Cholesterol 15mg
Iron 2.2mg
Sodium 942mg
Calcium 81mg

Gnocchi
(NYOH-kee) is the word for "dumplings." You can find commercial gnocchi in large supermarkets on the same aisle as dry pasta.

1	(16-ounce) package vacuum-packed potato gnocchi
1	tablespoon olive oil
1	ounce pancetta, finely diced
1	(8-ounce) package sliced baby portobello mushrooms
1½	cups chopped leek (about 1 medium)
1	teaspoon minced garlic
½	cup refrigerated light Alfredo sauce (such as Buitoni)
⅓	cup canned unsweetened pumpkin
¼	teaspoon salt
½	teaspoon freshly ground black pepper
½	cup fat-free, less-sodium chicken broth
¼	teaspoon rubbed sage

Fresh sage leaves (optional)

1. Cook gnocchi according to package directions, omitting salt and fat.

2. While gnocchi cooks, heat oil in a large nonstick skillet over medium-high heat. Add pancetta, and cook 3 minutes or until crisp. Add mushrooms, leek, and garlic; sauté 7 minutes or until tender. Reduce heat to low. Stir in Alfredo sauce, pumpkin, salt, and pepper; cook 2 minutes or until thoroughly heated. Stir in broth and sage.

3. Drain gnocchi. Add gnocchi to sauce in pan, and toss gently. Spoon into individual bowls, and garnish with sage leaves, if desired. Serve immediately. Yield: 4 servings (serving size: 1 cup).

PROSCIUTTO, MOZZARELLA, AND ARUGULA PANINI

pictured on page 80

The key to a good *panino* (singular) is high-quality bread, usually ciabatta, and fresh ingredients. Look for long, flat, rectangular-shaped loaves of ciabatta in your favorite deli or bakery.

4	teaspoons balsamic vinegar
2	teaspoons extravirgin olive oil
¼	teaspoon black pepper
1	garlic clove, minced
1	(9-ounce) loaf ciabatta, cut in half horizontally
16	very thin slices prosciutto (about 4 ounces)
4	(1-ounce) slices part-skim mozzarella cheese
8	(¼-inch-thick) slices tomato (1 medium tomato)
1	cup lightly packed trimmed arugula or spinach

Olive oil–flavored cooking spray

POINTS value:
8

exchanges:
2½ starch
2 medium-fat meat

per serving:
Calories 347
Fat 13.3g (saturated fat 5.1g)
Protein 19.5g
Carbohydrate 38g
Fiber 1.3g
Cholesterol 32mg
Iron 2.6mg
Sodium 1,017mg
Calcium 222mg

1. Combine first 4 ingredients in a small bowl; stir well with a whisk.

2. Brush cut sides of bread with vinaigrette. Arrange prosciutto and next 3 ingredients over bottom half of bread; replace top half of bread. Cut loaf in half crosswise, and coat with cooking spray.

3. Heat a large grill pan or nonstick skillet over medium heat. Add sandwich halves to pan. Place a heavy skillet on top of sandwiches to weigh them down. Cook 3 minutes on each side or until bread is toasted and cheese melts. Cut each sandwich half in half again to form 4 equal portions. Serve immediately. Yield: 4 servings (serving size: 1 sandwich).

Note: Focaccia may be substituted for ciabatta.

> *Panini* (pah-NEE-nee) translates as "rolls" or "little bread," but in Italy, the name is synonymous with sandwiches.

PIZZA QUATTRO STAGIONI

pictured on page 79

An Italian favorite, this pizza displays toppings that represent each season. In this version, artichokes stand for spring, pungent olives represent summer, woodsy mushrooms hint at autumn, and prosciutto makes a statement for winter.

POINTS value:
6

exchanges:
2 starch
1 high-fat meat

per serving:
Calories 273
Fat 10.3g (saturated fat 4.4g)
Protein 14.4g
Carbohydrate 30.7g
Fiber 2.6g
Cholesterol 23mg
Iron 2mg
Sodium 826mg
Calcium 233mg

> **Quattro stagioni** (KWAH-tro stah-gee-OH-nee) means "four seasons."

⅔ cup fat-free garlic-and-herb pasta sauce (such as Healthy Choice)
1 (14-ounce) cheese-flavored pizza crust (such as Boboli)
3 tablespoons grated fresh Parmesan cheese
¾ cup thinly sliced baby portobello mushrooms
2 tablespoons chopped fresh basil
1 (14-ounce) can quartered artichoke hearts, drained
1½ ounces thinly sliced prosciutto, cut into strips
6 kalamata or oil-cured olives, pitted and chopped
¾ cup (3 ounces) shredded part-skim mozzarella cheese
¾ cup (3 ounces) shredded fontina cheese

1. Preheat oven to 450°.
2. Spread pasta sauce over pizza crust, leaving a 1-inch border. Sprinkle with Parmesan cheese; top with mushrooms and next 4 ingredients. Sprinkle with mozzarella and fontina cheeses.
3. Place pizza on oven rack in center of oven. Bake at 450° for 10 minutes or until crust is golden and cheese melts. Remove to a cutting board; cut into 8 wedges. Yield: 8 servings (serving size: 1 slice).

CHICKEN CACCIATORE

This dish is the ultimate Italian comfort food. Serve it over pasta or polenta—both are good sauce catchers.

4	chicken thighs (about 1 pound 2 ounces), skinned
3	(8-ounce) bone-in chicken breast halves, skinned
⅛	teaspoon salt
¼	teaspoon black pepper
	Cooking spray
2	teaspoons olive oil
1¼	cups chopped onion
1	cup chopped red bell pepper
4	garlic cloves, minced
⅔	cup dry white wine or fat-free, less-sodium chicken broth
1	(28-ounce) can Italian-style tomatoes, undrained and chopped
⅓	cup pitted kalamata olives
½	cup fat-free, less-sodium chicken broth
2	teaspoons chopped fresh rosemary

POINTS value:
6

exchanges:
1 starch
5 very lean meat
1 fat

per serving:
Calories 296
Fat 7.9g (saturated fat 1.5g)
Protein 39.2g
Carbohydrate 13.5g
Fiber 2.5g
Cholesterol 111mg
Iron 5.5mg
Sodium 637mg
Calcium 95mg

1. Sprinkle chicken with salt and black pepper; coat both sides of chicken with cooking spray. Heat oil in a large nonstick skillet over medium-high heat. Add chicken; cook 5 minutes on each side or until browned. Remove chicken from pan.

2. Add onion, bell pepper, and garlic to pan; sauté over medium-high heat 5 minutes. Add chicken and wine to pan. Bring to a boil; reduce heat. Simmer 7 minutes or until wine almost evaporates, turning chicken and stirring occasionally.

3. Add tomatoes and remaining ingredients; bring to a boil. Cover; reduce heat. Simmer 20 minutes or until chicken is done. Place chicken on a platter; keep warm. Bring tomato mixture to a boil; boil 7 minutes or until sauce reduces moderately. Spoon sauce over chicken. Yield: 5 servings (serving size: 2 thighs or 1 breast half and about ¾ cup sauce).

Note: If buying only one cut of chicken, use 5 bone-in chicken breast halves, skinned, or 10 skinned chicken thighs.

Cacciatore (kah-chuh-TOR-ee) refers to a dish that's prepared in the "hunter's style." Differing legends revolve around this dish—some say the dish was cooked for the hunter as a send-off before a hunt; others believe the dish was created with the hunting bounty.

CHICKEN PARMESAN WITH RED-WINE PASTA SAUCE

pictured on page 113

POINTS value:
10

exchanges:
2 starch
2 vegetable
5½ very lean meat
1 fat

per serving:
Calories 462
Fat 11.3g (saturated fat 3.4g)
Protein 49.7g
Carbohydrate 37.8g
Fiber 3.4g
Cholesterol 111mg
Iron 3.7mg
Sodium 867mg
Calcium 196mg

4   ounces uncooked linguine
½   cup Italian-seasoned breadcrumbs
½   teaspoon dried Italian seasoning
4   (6-ounce) skinless, boneless chicken breast halves
1   large egg white, lightly beaten
½   teaspoon black pepper, divided
⅛   teaspoon salt
1   tablespoon olive oil
Dash of ground red pepper
½   cup dry red wine
2   cups light no sugar–added tomato-and-basil pasta sauce
4   teaspoons grated Parmesan cheese
½   cup (2 ounces) shredded part-skim mozzarella cheese
Basil sprigs (optional)

1. Cook pasta according to package directions, omitting salt and fat.
2. While pasta cooks, combine breadcrumbs and seasoning in a shallow dish. Dip chicken in egg white; sprinkle with ¼ teaspoon black pepper and salt, and dredge in breadcrumbs.
3. Heat oil in a large nonstick skillet over medium-high heat. Add chicken; cook 3 minutes on each side. Remove chicken from pan; keep warm. Add remaining ¼ teaspoon black pepper, red pepper, and wine to pan, scraping pan to loosen browned bits. Cook 1 minute. Add pasta sauce; cook 1 minute or until bubbly.
4. Arrange chicken over sauce; top each breast half with a spoonful of sauce, and sprinkle with cheeses. Cover, reduce heat, and simmer 5 minutes or until chicken is done.
5. Drain pasta. Serve chicken and sauce over pasta. Garnish with basil, if desired. Yield: 4 servings (serving size: ½ cup pasta, 1 chicken breast half, about ⅓ cup sauce, 1 teaspoon Parmesan cheese, and 2 tablespoons mozzarella cheese).

CHICKEN SALTIMBOCCA

This traditional Roman dish is usually made with veal, but it works just as well with chicken.

8   (6-ounce) skinless, boneless chicken breast cutlets
¼   teaspoon salt
¼   teaspoon freshly ground black pepper
8   very thin slices prosciutto (about 2 ounces)
16 large fresh sage leaves
2   teaspoons olive oil
½   cup dry white wine
½   cup fat-free, less-sodium chicken broth
½   teaspoon chopped fresh sage

1. Sprinkle chicken evenly with salt and pepper. Place 1 slice prosciutto and 2 sage leaves on top of each chicken cutlet. Roll up, and secure with a wooden pick.
2. Heat oil in a large nonstick skillet over medium-high heat. Add chicken rolls, and cook 6 minutes, turning to brown on all sides. Remove chicken from pan. Add wine and chicken broth to pan; bring to a boil. Cook 2 minutes or until slightly reduced. Reduce heat to medium.
3. Return chicken and any juices to pan; stir in chopped sage. Cover and cook over medium heat 20 minutes or until chicken is done.
4. Remove wooden picks from chicken; cut each roll into ½-inch-thick slices. Spoon sauce over chicken. Yield: 8 servings (serving size: 1 chicken roll and 4 teaspoons sauce).

POINTS value:
5

exchanges:
5 very lean meat
½ fat

per serving:
Calories 208
Fat 5.8g (saturated fat 1.5g)
Protein 36.2g
Carbohydrate 0.5g
Fiber 0g
Cholesterol 98mg
Iron 1.3mg
Sodium 298mg
Calcium 25mg

Saltimbocca
(sahl-tihm-BOH-kah) means "to leap in the mouth." This dish is so named because the flavors are so lively.

LEMON AND HERB–ROASTED CHICKEN THIGHS

We like using chicken thighs for this recipe because the meat is more flavorful and stands up to the robustness of the marinade. With a quick one-hour marinating period, this chicken dish received top ratings from our taste-testing panel, but you may marinate the chicken all day or overnight if you prefer.

POINTS value:
7

exchanges:
4 medium-fat meat

per serving:
Calories 300
Fat 17.9g (saturated fat 4.3g)
Protein 30.8g
Carbohydrate 2.7g
Fiber 0.6g
Cholesterol 112mg
Iron 1.8mg
Sodium 288mg
Calcium 35mg

2 tablespoons chopped fresh oregano
2 tablespoons chopped fresh rosemary
1 tablespoon chopped fresh thyme
1 teaspoon grated fresh lemon rind
¼ cup fresh lemon juice
1½ tablespoons olive oil
¼ teaspoon crushed red pepper
¼ teaspoon freshly ground black pepper
⅛ teaspoon salt
4 garlic cloves, minced (about 2 tablespoons)
¼ cup coarsely chopped green olives (such as Sicilian)
8 (3-ounce) skinless, boneless chicken thighs
Cooking spray

1. Combine first 10 ingredients in a large zip-top plastic bag. Remove 2 tablespoons marinade mixture; place in a small bowl, and stir in olives. Set aside.
2. Add chicken to remaining marinade, tossing well to coat. Seal bag, and marinate in refrigerator 1 hour.
3. Preheat oven to 450°.
4. Remove chicken from marinade; discard marinade. Place chicken on a jelly-roll pan coated with cooking spray. Bake at 450° for 25 minutes or until done. Place chicken on a serving platter. Spoon reserved olive mixture evenly over chicken. Yield: 4 servings (serving size: 2 thighs and 1½ tablespoons olive mixture).

CANNELLINI BEANS WITH SAUSAGES AND SAGE

Dinner doesn't get any easier than this hearty meal. From start to finish, it's prepared in one skillet, so there's very little cleanup involved. And you don't have to worry about any side dishes because it's a complete meal all in itself. We used sweet turkey Italian sausage, but you can spice things up a bit with hot turkey Italian sausage. If you're watching your sodium intake, look for no salt–added tomatoes and white beans; this will reduce the amount of sodium to 1,067 milligrams per serving.

Cooking spray
1½ pounds sweet lean turkey Italian sausage (5 links)
2 cups diced onion
3 garlic cloves, minced
2 (15-ounce) cans cannellini beans or other white beans, rinsed and drained
1 (28-ounce) can diced tomatoes with basil and garlic, undrained
½ teaspoon fennel seeds
1 tablespoon finely chopped fresh sage

1. Heat a large, deep skillet over medium heat; coat pan with cooking spray. Add sausage links, and cook 5 minutes or until browned on all sides. Remove sausage links from pan, and set aside.
2. Add onion and garlic to pan; sauté over medium heat 5 minutes or until tender. Stir in beans, tomatoes, and fennel seeds. Bring to a boil; return sausage to pan. Reduce heat and simmer, uncovered, 20 minutes or until sausage is done. Remove from heat; stir in sage. Yield: 5 servings (serving size: 1 sausage link and 1 cup tomato-bean mixture).

POINTS value:
8

exchanges:
1 starch
4 vegetable
3 medium-fat meat

per serving:
Calories 381
Fat 13g (saturated fat 3.1g)
Protein 28.9g
Carbohydrate 36.8g
Fiber 6.6g
Cholesterol 81mg
Iron 5.4mg
Sodium 1,774mg
Calcium 183mg

TURKEY TONNATO

Turkey served with tuna sauce certainly isn't a common flavor combo for the American palate, but give it a try. The pairing of flavors truly is tasty. It's traditionally served chilled, but we served the sauce at room temperature over warm turkey. The sauce is delicious over chicken, too.

POINTS value:
7

exchanges:
5½ very lean meat

per serving:
Calories 293
Fat 14.1g (saturated fat 2.2g)
Protein 39.6g
Carbohydrate 3.2g
Fiber 0.1g
Cholesterol 73mg
Iron 2.1mg
Sodium 797mg
Calcium 8mg

> **Tonnato** (tohn-NAH-toh) means "tuna sauce" in Italian.

2	(¾-pound) turkey tenderloins
1	tablespoon olive oil
2	tablespoons dried Italian seasoning
½	teaspoon salt
¼	teaspoon white pepper
1¼	cups fat-free, less-sodium chicken broth, divided
½	cup light mayonnaise
2	tablespoons fresh lemon juice
1	tablespoon capers
1	teaspoon caper juice
1	(6-ounce) can albacore tuna in water, drained
1	canned anchovy fillet
1	tablespoon chopped fresh flat-leaf parsley

1. Preheat oven to 350°.

2. Place turkey tenderloins in an 8-inch square baking dish; rub with oil. Sprinkle tenderloins evenly with Italian seasoning, salt, and pepper. Pour 1 cup chicken broth into dish. Bake, uncovered, at 350° for 35 to 40 minutes or until a thermometer registers 170°. Let stand 10 minutes.

3. While turkey stands, place remaining ¼ cup broth, mayonnaise, and next 5 ingredients in a food processor; process until smooth. Remove turkey from dish; discard broth. Cut tenderloins diagonally into 1-inch-thick medallions. Spoon sauce over sliced turkey, and sprinkle with parsley. Serve warm. Yield: 5 servings (serving size: about 4 ounces turkey and ¼ cup sauce).

Pasta & Sauces

ORZO WITH BASIL, ORANGE, AND PINE NUTS

At first glance, this recipe may look like any other simple side dish, but the flavor is anything but simple. Orzo cooks in vegetable broth to boost the flavor before it's tossed with a garlic-infused orange-juice reduction and fresh basil. At the end of taste testing, there wasn't a piece of orzo left in the bowl, and the recipe received our highest rating.

POINTS value:
4

exchanges:
1½ starch
1½ fat

per serving:
Calories 183
Fat 7.2g (saturated fat 2.2g)
Protein 5.9g
Carbohydrate 23.2g
Fiber 1.2g
Cholesterol 7mg
Iron 0.4mg
Sodium 487mg
Calcium 83mg

2   (14-ounce) cans vegetable broth (such as Swanson)
1½   cups uncooked orzo (rice-shaped pasta)
2   tablespoons olive oil
1   tablespoon butter
1   tablespoon grated fresh orange rind
3   garlic cloves, minced
¾   cup fresh orange juice
⅓   cup chopped fresh basil
¾   cup shredded fresh Parmigiano-Reggiano cheese
2   tablespoons pine nuts, toasted
¼   teaspoon freshly ground black pepper

1. Bring broth to a boil in a medium saucepan. Add pasta; reduce heat to medium, and cook 9 to 12 minutes or until tender. Drain.

2. While pasta cooks, combine oil and next 3 ingredients in a medium saucepan; cook over medium-low heat 3 to 5 minutes or until butter melts and garlic is soft and fragrant, stirring often. Increase heat to medium-high. Add orange juice; cook 3 minutes or until juice reduces slightly, stirring often. Remove from heat; stir in basil. Add pasta to pan, tossing to coat. Stir in cheese, pine nuts, and pepper. Yield: 10 servings (serving size: ½ cup).

Note: Toast the pine nuts in a small skillet over medium heat for 1 minute until they are fragrant and begin to take on a golden hue. Transfer to a plate to cool quickly. A Microplane® grater works wonders to get the finest zest from the oranges. Be sure to remove the zest before you juice them.

LEMON SPAGHETTI

Light and lemony, this pasta pairs perfectly with grilled fish and chicken. Don't worry if you forget to reserve some of the pasta water because tap water works just fine.

6	ounces uncooked spaghetti
1	teaspoon fresh thyme leaves
1	teaspoon grated fresh lemon rind
2	tablespoons fresh lemon juice
2	teaspoons olive oil
2	teaspoons capers
¼	teaspoon salt
¼	teaspoon freshly ground black pepper
2	tablespoons grated fresh Parmesan cheese, divided

POINTS value:
3

exchanges:
1½ starch

per serving:
Calories 128
Fat 2.4g (saturated fat 0.6g)
Protein 4.3g
Carbohydrate 21.9g
Fiber 0.8g
Cholesterol 1mg
Iron 1.2mg
Sodium 153mg
Calcium 26mg

1. Cook pasta according to package directions, omitting salt and fat.

2. While pasta cooks, combine thyme and next 6 ingredients in a large bowl.

3. Drain pasta, reserving 2 tablespoons pasta water. Add pasta, reserved pasta water, and 1 tablespoon cheese to lemon mixture in bowl; toss well. Sprinkle with remaining 1 tablespoon cheese. Serve immediately. Yield: 6 servings (serving size: ½ cup).

LINGUINE WITH CREMA DI NOCI

Tossing in some chopped walnuts adds extra flavor and a nice crunch to this creamy dish.

POINTS value:
7

exchanges:
3 starch
2 fat

per serving:
Calories 330
Fat 11.2g (saturated fat 2.4g)
Protein 12.7g
Carbohydrate 46.2g
Fiber 2.7g
Cholesterol 9mg
Iron 2.3mg
Sodium 384mg
Calcium 129mg

Crema di noci
(KREH-mah dee NOH-chee) means "cream of walnut." Toasted walnuts are puréed into butter as a base for this pasta sauce.

---

8 ounces uncooked linguine
½ cup walnut halves
½ teaspoon salt
2 garlic cloves, peeled and halved
½ cup 2% reduced-fat milk
¼ teaspoon freshly ground black pepper
¼ cup grated fresh Romano cheese

1. Preheat oven to 350°.
2. Cook pasta according to package directions, omitting salt and fat.
3. While pasta cooks, place walnuts in a single layer on a baking sheet. Bake at 350° for 8 minutes or until toasted. Place ⅓ cup hot walnuts, salt, and garlic in a food processor; process until nuts are finely ground. Microwave milk at HIGH 1 minute or until hot. Add hot milk to food processor; process until smooth. Chop remaining walnuts.
4. Drain pasta, reserving ¼ cup pasta water. Combine pasta, walnut cream, chopped walnuts, and pepper in a bowl; toss to coat. If necessary, add reserved pasta water, 1 tablespoon at a time, to thin walnut cream. Sprinkle with Romano cheese. Serve immediately. Yield: 4 servings (serving size: 1 cup).

prep: 8 minutes • **cook:** 30 minutes

GARDEN LINGUINE WITH PESTO

Italy's Liguria region is widely known for fresh basil pesto. It's no wonder this wonderfully aromatic no-cook sauce is one of the most popular dishes in Genoa. After tasting this hearty meatless main dish, pesto will be a favorite with your family, too.

¼   pound small red potatoes, cut into ½-inch cubes
¼   pound fresh green beans, trimmed and halved
8   ounces uncooked linguine
¼   cup grated fresh Parmesan cheese, divided
2   cups packed fresh basil leaves
2   tablespoons pine nuts, toasted
2   garlic cloves, peeled and halved
3   tablespoons extravirgin olive oil
½   teaspoon salt
¼   teaspoon freshly ground black pepper

POINTS value:
7

exchanges:
2½ starch
2½ fat

per serving:
Calories 311
Fat 12.7g (saturated fat 2.2g)
Protein 9.6g
Carbohydrate 40.8g
Fiber 3.5g
Cholesterol 4mg
Iron 2.7mg
Sodium 300mg
Calcium 96mg

1. Cook potatoes in a large pot of boiling water 5 minutes or just until tender. Remove potatoes with a slotted spoon; place in a large bowl. Add green beans to boiling water, and cook 3 minutes or until crisp-tender. Remove green beans with a slotted spoon; place in bowl with potatoes. Add pasta to boiling water, and cook 9 minutes or until pasta is done.

2. While vegetables and pasta cook, combine 2 tablespoons Parmesan cheese and next 3 ingredients in a food processor or blender. With processor on, slowly pour oil through food chute; process until well blended.

3. Drain pasta, reserving ⅓ cup cooking liquid. Add pasta to bowl with potatoes and green beans. Sprinkle with salt and pepper. Add reserved ⅓ cup cooking liquid to food processor; process until well blended. Add pesto to pasta mixture; toss gently to coat. Spoon pasta into individual bowls, and sprinkle with remaining 2 tablespoons cheese. Yield: 5 servings (serving size: 1 cup pasta mixture and about 1¼ teaspoons cheese).

ROASTED-ASPARAGUS PASTA PRIMAVERA
pictured on page 114

We streamlined this recipe to focus on three star vegetables instead of a garden variety. Roasting the vegetables intensifies their flavor and also simplifies the preparation and cleanup. Look for precut matchstick carrots in the produce section of your grocery store. A small amount of cream per serving is the ticket to an incredibly rich and tasty, yet healthful, pasta dish.

POINTS value:
7

exchanges:
2 starch
1½ vegetable
2½ fat

per serving:
Calories 317
Fat 14.1g (saturated fat 7.8g)
Protein 10.6g
Carbohydrate 37.5g
Fiber 3.7g
Cholesterol 48mg
Iron 2.8mg
Sodium 359mg
Calcium 153mg

1½	pounds asparagus spears
1	cup matchstick carrots
½	medium sweet onion, halved and thinly sliced (about 1 cup)
1	teaspoon bottled minced garlic
1	teaspoon olive oil
½	teaspoon salt
¼	teaspoon freshly ground black pepper
1	pint grape tomatoes
8	ounces uncooked penne (tube-shaped pasta)
¾	cup whipping cream
⅔	cup grated fresh Parmesan cheese

1. Preheat oven to 450°.

2. Snap off tough ends of asparagus, and cut asparagus into 1-inch pieces. Combine asparagus and next 3 ingredients in a large roasting pan. Drizzle with olive oil, and sprinkle with salt and pepper; toss gently to coat. Bake at 450° for 15 minutes or until vegetables begin to brown, stirring vegetables after 10 minutes. Add tomatoes, and cook an additional 5 minutes.

3. While vegetables roast, cook pasta according to package directions, omitting salt and fat. Drain well, reserving ⅓ cup pasta water.

4. Combine vegetables, pasta, reserved ⅓ cup pasta water, and whipping cream; toss gently to coat. Sprinkle with cheese. Serve immediately. Yield: 6 servings (serving size: 1⅓ cups).

LINGUINE WITH CLAM SAUCE

This dish makes the most of a well-stocked pantry. In the time it takes to cook the pasta, you'll have a light and healthy entrée on the table.

8   ounces uncooked linguine
2   (6½-ounce) cans minced clams, undrained
1½   tablespoons olive oil
⅓   cup minced shallots (about 2 medium)
1   tablespoon bottled minced garlic
½   cup dry white wine or clam juice
2   teaspoons lemon juice
½   teaspoon black pepper
¼   teaspoon salt
¼   teaspoon crushed red pepper
⅓   cup minced fresh parsley

1. Cook pasta according to package directions, omitting salt and fat.
2. While pasta cooks, drain clams, reserving ½ cup clam juice. Heat oil in a large nonstick skillet over medium-high heat. Add shallots and garlic; sauté 2 minutes or until shallots are tender. Add reserved ½ cup clam juice, wine, and next 4 ingredients; bring to a boil. Stir in clams and parsley. Reduce heat, and simmer 3 minutes.
3. Drain pasta. Combine pasta and clam mixture; toss well. Yield: 4 servings (serving size: about 1 cup).

Note: If substituting additional clam juice for dry white wine, the sodium content will be 512 milligrams per serving.

POINTS value:
6

exchanges:
3 starch
1 fat

per serving:
Calories 293
Fat 6.5g (saturated fat 1g)
Protein 11g
Carbohydrate 47.1g
Fiber 2.2g
Cholesterol 7mg
Iron 3.1mg
Sodium 450mg
Calcium 30mg

prep: 25 minutes • cook: 25 minutes

SPAGHETTI AND MEATBALLS
pictured on cover

POINTS value:
8

exchanges:
2 starch
4 vegetable
2 lean meat

per serving:
Calories 387
Fat 7.9g (saturated fat 2.4g)
Protein 30.9g
Carbohydrate 49.7g
Fiber 2g
Cholesterol 82mg
Iron 5.1mg
Sodium 940mg
Calcium 117mg

1   (1.5-ounce) slice whole wheat bread
1   garlic clove
½   small onion, cut into 3 wedges
½   cup parsley leaves
1   pound ground round
2   (4-ounce) links sweet turkey Italian sausage, casings removed
¼   cup grated Parmesan cheese
¼   cup fat-free, less-sodium chicken broth
1   large egg
½   teaspoon salt
½   teaspoon black pepper
¼   teaspoon crushed red pepper
Cooking spray
12   ounces uncooked spaghetti
2   (25.5-ounce) jars Italian herb pasta sauce (we tested with Muir Glen Organic)
Grated Parmesan cheese (optional)

1. Preheat oven to 400°.
2. Place bread in a food processor; pulse 10 times or until coarse crumbs measure ½ cup. Transfer to a bowl; set aside.
3. Place garlic, onion, and parsley in processor; pulse 20 seconds or until chopped. Add breadcrumbs, ground round, and next 7 ingredients. Pulse 1 minute or until mixture is combined, stopping frequently to scrape down sides.
4. Line a broiler pan with foil. Shape meat mixture into 48 (1½-inch) balls. Place meatballs on broiler rack coated with cooking spray. Bake at 400° for 12 minutes or until meatballs are no longer pink in center.
5. While meatballs cook, cook pasta according to package directions, omitting salt and fat.
6. Bring pasta sauce to a simmer in a large saucepan. Add meatballs, and simmer 10 minutes or until sauce reaches desired consistency. Serve over spaghetti. Serve with additional Parmesan cheese, if desired. Yield: 8 servings (serving size: ¾ cup pasta and 1 cup plus 2 tablespoons sauce).

PASTA ALLA CARBONARA

You'll fall in love with the smoky flavor of bacon combined with sharp Parmesan cheese and garlic—all tossed with pasta and thickened with egg. Make this classic pasta dish kid-friendly by omitting the crushed red pepper.

½	cup grated Parmesan cheese, divided
⅓	cup plus 2 tablespoons 1% low-fat milk
¼	cup egg substitute
½	teaspoon salt
¼	teaspoon black pepper
¼	teaspoon crushed red pepper
8	ounces uncooked linguine
6	center-cut bacon slices
1	cup chopped onion (1 small)
3	garlic cloves, minced

1. Combine ⅓ cup Parmesan cheese and next 5 ingredients in a bowl; stir well, and set aside.

2. Cook pasta according to package directions, omitting salt and fat.

3. While pasta cooks, cook bacon in a large nonstick skillet over medium-high heat until crisp. Remove bacon from pan, reserving 2 teaspoons drippings in pan. Crumble bacon, and set aside. Add onion and garlic to drippings in pan; sauté 5 minutes or until tender.

4. Drain pasta; return to pan. Add egg mixture, bacon, and onion mixture to hot pasta; toss gently to coat. Place over low heat, and cook 1 minute. Spoon pasta into individual bowls, and sprinkle with remaining Parmesan cheese. Serve immediately. Yield: 5 servings (serving size: 1 cup pasta mixture and about 1½ teaspoons cheese).

POINTS value:
6

exchanges:
2½ starch
1 medium-fat meat

per serving:
Calories 281
Fat 7.6g (saturated fat 3.4g)
Protein 14.1g
Carbohydrate 39.5g
Fiber 2g
Cholesterol 17mg
Iron 2mg
Sodium 550mg
Calcium 140mg

Carbonara (kar-boh-NAH-rah) literally translates as the "charcoal maker's wife." Word has it that the charcoal sellers from Abruzzo introduced this dish to the city of Rome.

CONCHIGLIE WITH AMATRICIANA SAUCE

The graceful concave shape of seashell pasta gathers and holds every drop of this rustic, smoky tomato sauce. However, this easy-to-make sauce complements any shape of pasta.

POINTS value:
4

exchanges:
2 starch
1 vegetable
½ fat

per serving:
Calories 206
Fat 3.5g (saturated fat 1.4g)
Protein 7.6g
Carbohydrate 36g
Fiber 3.2g
Cholesterol 7mg
Iron 1.8mg
Sodium 342mg
Calcium 47mg

Amatriciana
(ah-mah-tree-CHAH-nah), a tomato-based sauce with pancetta, garlic, and crushed red pepper, is named for the small town of Amatrice. It's perfect served over **conchiglie** *(con-KEE-lyay).*

⅓	cup diced pancetta
1	medium onion, cut in half crosswise and sliced into ¼-inch wedges
3	garlic cloves, minced
1	(28-ounce) can diced tomatoes, undrained
¼	teaspoon crushed red pepper
¼	teaspoon salt
12	ounces uncooked conchiglie rigate (small seashell pasta)
8	teaspoons grated fresh Parmigiano-Reggiano cheese

1. Heat a large saucepan over medium-high heat. Add pancetta; sauté 2 minutes or until browned. Add onion and garlic; reduce heat to medium, and cook 7 minutes or until onion is lightly browned. Add tomatoes, red pepper, and salt; simmer, uncovered, 30 minutes.

2. While sauce simmers, cook pasta according to package directions, omitting salt and fat. Drain pasta, and return to pan. Add sauce, and toss to coat. Spoon pasta into individual bowls, and sprinkle with cheese. Yield: 8 servings (serving size: 1 cup pasta and 1 teaspoon cheese).

ANGEL HAIR PASTA WITH PROSCIUTTO AND MUSHROOM CREAM SAUCE

In Italy, pasta dishes are commonly tossed with a light dressing rather than a heavy sauce. When served this way, all components of the dish play an important role in both flavor and texture.

1 (9-ounce) package refrigerated angel hair pasta
Olive oil–flavored cooking spray
1 (8-ounce) package mushrooms, quartered
¼ cup julienne-cut ready-to-eat sun-dried tomatoes (such as California Sun Dry)
1½ tablespoons minced garlic (about 5 cloves)
2 ounces very thinly sliced prosciutto (about 4 slices), sliced crosswise into ½-inch strips
½ cup dry white wine or fat-free, less-sodium chicken broth
½ cup fat-free, less-sodium chicken broth
1 cup frozen baby green peas, thawed
½ teaspoon freshly ground black pepper
1 (10-ounce) container refrigerated light Alfredo sauce (such as Buitoni)
¼ cup shredded fresh Parmesan cheese

1. Cook pasta according to package directions, omitting salt and fat.
2. While pasta cooks, heat a large nonstick skillet over medium-high heat. Coat pan with cooking spray. Add mushrooms, and sauté 5 minutes or until tender. Add sun-dried tomatoes, garlic, and prosciutto; sauté 2 minutes. Add wine and broth; bring to a boil. Boil 3 minutes or until liquid is reduced to ½ cup. Stir in peas, pepper, and Alfredo sauce.
3. Drain pasta, and return to pan. Add sauce, and toss gently to coat. Spoon pasta into individual bowls, and sprinkle with cheese. Serve immediately. Yield: 4 servings (serving size: 1½ cups pasta and 1 tablespoon cheese).

POINTS value:
8

exchanges:
3 starch
1½ vegetable
1 high-fat meat

per serving:
Calories 377
Fat 10.5g (saturated fat 5.4g)
Protein 20.9g
Carbohydrate 51.4g
Fiber 5.4g
Cholesterol 35mg
Iron 2.9mg
Sodium 965mg
Calcium 200mg

TORTELLINI IN BRODO

This dish is traditionally served as a special Christmas treat, but refrigerated tortellini and canned broth create a meal that's ready in mere minutes any night of the week. Arugula and two types of pepper add a spicy kick to the broth. Tone down the heat by omitting the crushed red pepper and substituting 2 cups of chopped fresh spinach for the arugula.

POINTS value:
5

exchanges:
2 starch
1½ vegetable
1 fat

per serving:
Calories 233
Fat 4.8g (saturated fat 1.9g)
Protein 11.9g
Carbohydrate 36.6g
Fiber 2.7g
Cholesterol 21mg
Iron 0.8mg
Sodium 686mg
Calcium 80mg

Brodo (BROH-doh) is the Italian word for broth.

2¾ cups fat-free, less-sodium chicken broth
¼ teaspoon freshly ground black pepper
¼ teaspoon crushed red pepper
1 (9-ounce) package fresh three-cheese tortellini
1 (5-ounce) bag fresh arugula or spinach
1 cup coarsely chopped tomato (about 1 medium)
4 teaspoons shredded fresh Parmesan cheese

1. Bring first 3 ingredients to a simmer in a medium saucepan. Add tortellini, and cook the amount of time given by the package directions; do not drain.
2. Remove from heat; stir in arugula. Let stand 1 minute or until arugula wilts.
3. Ladle 1 cup broth-tortellini mixture into each of 4 bowls. Top each with ¼ cup tomato and 1 teaspoon Parmesan cheese. Yield: 4 servings.

ORECCHIETTE WITH SPICY TURKEY SAUSAGE AND BROCCOLI RABE

Boiling the broccoli rabe with the pasta tones down the bitter flavor of this dark green, leafy vegetable. Hot sausage and crushed red pepper add a kick of heat that can be tempered by using sweet turkey Italian sausage and less red pepper.

¾ pound broccoli rabe (rapini)
2 quarts water
1¾ cups (6 ounces) uncooked orecchiette ("little ears" pasta)
½ pound hot turkey Italian sausage
Cooking spray
½ cup chopped onion
2 garlic cloves, minced
½ cup fat-free, less-sodium chicken broth
¼ teaspoon crushed red pepper
¼ teaspoon freshly ground black pepper
⅛ teaspoon salt
1 pint grape tomatoes, halved
2 tablespoons grated fresh Parmesan cheese

1. Thinly slice green leaves of broccoli rabe, and cut stems into 2-inch pieces.
2. Bring 2 quarts water to a boil in a Dutch oven. Add pasta; cook 6 minutes. Add broccoli rabe leaves and stems; cook 5 minutes or until tender.
3. While pasta and broccoli rabe cook, remove casings from sausage. Heat a large nonstick skillet over medium-high heat. Coat pan with cooking spray. Add onion and garlic; sauté 3 minutes or until tender. Add sausage; cook 7 minutes or until browned, stirring to crumble. Add broth and next 3 ingredients; bring to a boil. Drain pasta and broccoli rabe; stir hot cooked pasta, broccoli rabe, and tomatoes into sausage mixture; cook 1 minute or until thoroughly heated. Sprinkle with cheese; toss well. Yield: 6 servings (serving size: 1½ cups).

POINTS value:
4

exchanges:
1½ starch
1 vegetable
1 medium-fat meat

per serving:
Calories 210
Fat 5.1g (saturated fat 1.7g)
Protein 13.5g
Carbohydrate 28.2g
Fiber 1.5g
Cholesterol 24mg
Iron 2.4mg
Sodium 386mg
Calcium 60mg

> *Orecchiette*
> *(oh-rayk-kee-EHT-tay), a pasta originally from the Puglia region, is named for its resemblance to "little ears."*

GARLICKY RIGATONI WITH GORGONZOLA

Gorgonzola can range in flavor from mild to extremely powerful. Because cooking diminishes the flavor of the cheese, it doesn't overpower this dish. Instead, it lends just the right bite to this hearty pasta side dish to make it an excellent accompaniment to a grilled steak.

POINTS value:
5

exchanges:
2½ starch
1 fat

per serving:
Calories 238
Fat 5.6g (saturated fat 3.7g)
Protein 11.3g
Carbohydrate 35.7g
Fiber 1.7g
Cholesterol 17mg
Iron 1.4mg
Sodium 386mg
Calcium 204mg

12 ounces uncooked rigatoni (tube-shaped pasta)
⅓ cup all-purpose flour
2 cups fat-free milk
1½ cups fat-free half-and-half
1 teaspoon butter
10 garlic cloves, finely chopped
1 cup (4 ounces) crumbed Gorgonzola cheese, divided
½ teaspoon salt
¼ teaspoon black pepper
⅓ cup grated Romano cheese
Cooking spray

1. Preheat oven to 425°.

2. Cook pasta according to package directions, omitting salt and fat.

3. While pasta cooks, place flour in a medium bowl. Gradually add milk and half-and-half, stirring with a whisk until well blended. Melt butter in a large saucepan over medium heat. Add garlic; sauté 1 minute or until golden brown. Add milk mixture, and bring to a boil, stirring frequently with whisk. Stir in ½ cup Gorgonzola cheese, salt, and pepper. Reduce heat, and simmer, uncovered, 2 minutes or until cheese melts.

4. Drain pasta, and return to pan. Add Gorgonzola sauce and Romano cheese; toss gently to coat. Spoon pasta mixture into an 11 x 7–inch baking dish coated with cooking spray; sprinkle with remaining ½ cup Gorgonzola cheese. Bake, uncovered, at 425° for 27 minutes or until bubbly and lightly browned. Yield: 10 servings (serving size: about ¾ cup).

Chicken Parmesan with Red-Wine
Pasta Sauce, page 94

**Roasted-Asparagus Pasta
Primavera, page 104**

Puttanesca Sauce, page 128

Penne con Salsicce

PENNE CON SALSICCE

pictured on facing page

Any tube-shaped pasta will work well to hold the piquant *salsicce* (sausage)
for a burst of flavor with every bite.

8 ounces uncooked penne (tube-shaped pasta)
8 ounces hot turkey Italian sausage
1 teaspoon olive oil
½ cup vertically sliced onion (about ½ medium)
2 garlic cloves, thinly sliced
1 (14.5-ounce) can diced tomatoes with basil, garlic, and oregano, undrained
¼ cup dry red wine or fat-free, less-sodium beef broth
2 tablespoons tomato paste with Italian herbs
½ teaspoon crushed red pepper
½ teaspoon dried basil
½ teaspoon dried oregano
¼ teaspoon salt
¼ teaspoon freshly ground black pepper
Cooking spray
1 cup (4 ounces) finely shredded part-skim mozzarella cheese

POINTS value:
6

exchanges:
2 starch
1½ vegetable
2 lean meat

per serving:
Calories 307
Fat 8.4g (saturated fat 3.3g)
Protein 19.1g
Carbohydrate 38.4g
Fiber 2.2g
Cholesterol 44mg
Iron 3.4mg
Sodium 889mg
Calcium 181mg

> **Salsicce** (sahl-SE-chay) is traditionally pork sausage, but we've substituted turkey Italian sausage in this recipe.

1. Cook pasta according to package directions, omitting salt and fat.
2. While pasta cooks, remove casings from sausage. Heat oil in a large nonstick skillet over medium-high heat. Add onion and garlic; sauté 2 minutes or until tender. Add sausage; cook 7 minutes or until browned, stirring to crumble. Stir in tomatoes and next 7 ingredients. Cover, reduce heat to medium–low, and simmer 10 minutes, stirring occasionally.
3. Preheat broiler.
4. Drain pasta, and return to pan. Add sauce, and toss gently to coat. Spoon mixture into an 11 x 7–inch baking dish coated with cooking spray. Sprinkle with cheese. Broil 2 minutes or until cheese melts. Serve immediately. Yield: 6 servings (serving size: 1¼ cups).

BAKED RIGATONI WITH SAUSAGE AND MIXED PEPPERS

A *balsamella* (bal-sah-MEHL-ah) is a white sauce made from milk and flour. It's a staple of Italian cooking and is often used as a topping for baked pasta dishes. It adds creamy richness to this dish and keeps the pasta moist as it bakes.

POINTS value:
6

exchanges:
3 starch
2 vegetable
1 fat

per serving:
Calories 341
Fat 5.5g (saturated fat 1.8g)
Protein 17g
Carbohydrate 54.2g
Fiber 4.3g
Cholesterol 25mg
Iron 3.1mg
Sodium 707mg
Calcium 162mg

16   ounces uncooked rigatoni (tube-shaped pasta)
8   ounces hot turkey Italian sausage
Cooking spray
1¾   cups chopped onion (about 1 large)
1   medium green bell pepper, seeded and cut into strips
1   medium yellow bell pepper, seeded and cut into strips
1   medium red bell pepper, seeded and cut into strips
6   garlic cloves, minced
1   (26-ounce) jar marinara sauce with Burgundy wine (such as Bertolli)
½   cup all-purpose flour
½   teaspoon salt
2   cups fat-free milk
½   cup plus 2 tablespoons grated fresh Parmigiano-Reggiano cheese, divided

1. Preheat oven to 425°.

2. Cook pasta according to package directions, omitting salt and fat.

3. While pasta cooks, remove casings from sausage. Heat a large nonstick skillet over medium-high heat. Coat pan with cooking spray. Add sausage and onion; cook until sausage is browned, stirring to crumble. Add bell peppers and garlic; cook 3 minutes, stirring frequently. Stir in marinara sauce; cover, reduce heat, and simmer 10 minutes or until peppers are tender.

4. Drain pasta, and return to pan. Add pepper mixture; toss gently to coat. Divide pasta mixture evenly between 2 (11 x 7–inch) baking dishes coated with cooking spray.

5. Place flour and salt in a medium saucepan. Gradually add milk, stirring with a whisk until well blended. Bring to a boil over medium heat, and cook 3 minutes or until thick, stirring constantly with a whisk. Remove from heat; stir in ½ cup cheese. Pour 1 cup white sauce over each casserole; sprinkle each with 1 tablespoon cheese. Bake at 425° for 20 minutes or until lightly browned and bubbly. Yield: 10 servings (serving size: about 1 cup).

Freezer Friendly: This recipe makes two casseroles— enough for a crowd. Or serve one for a family meal and freeze the other for later. When you're ready, simply bake the frozen casserole, covered, at 425° for 30 minutes; uncover and bake an additional 30 minutes.

MANICOTTI FLORENTINE

Freeze leftovers in individual portions so each serving can be quickly reheated in the microwave. Microwave frozen manicotti, uncovered, at HIGH 4 to 5 minutes or until hot, rotating every minute.

POINTS value:
7

exchanges:
2 starch
2 vegetable
2½ lean meat

per serving:
Calories 367
Fat 10.3g (saturated fat 6.3g)
Protein 28.5g
Carbohydrate 41.8g
Fiber 5.2g
Cholesterol 43mg
Iron 3.3mg
Sodium 868mg
Calcium 433mg

1   (8-ounce) package uncooked manicotti shells
1   cup (4 ounces) shredded part-skim mozzarella cheese, divided
½   cup grated fresh Parmesan cheese, divided
2   (10-ounce) packages frozen chopped spinach, thawed, drained, and squeezed dry
1½ cups 2% low-fat cottage cheese
¾   cup chopped green onions (about 6 onions)
1   teaspoon lemon pepper
½   teaspoon dried oregano
¼   teaspoon garlic powder
1   (15-ounce) container part-skim ricotta cheese
3   large egg whites
1   (26-ounce) jar garlic-and-herb pasta sauce (such as Healthy Choice)
Cooking spray
2   tablespoons chopped fresh parsley

1. Preheat over to 350°.
2. Cook pasta according to package directions, omitting salt and fat.
3. While pasta cooks, combine ½ cup mozzarella, ¼ cup Parmesan, spinach, and next 7 ingredients in a large bowl; stir well. Drain pasta, and rinse with cold water to prevent sticking; drain. Spoon spinach mixture evenly into pasta shells (about ⅓ cup filling in each).
4. Spoon ½ cup pasta sauce in bottom of a 13 x 9–inch baking dish coated with cooking spray. Arrange stuffed pasta shells over sauce in dish; top with remaining sauce. Sprinkle evenly with remaining ½ cup mozzarella, remaining ¼ cup Parmesan, and parsley. Cover and bake at 350° for 45 minutes or until thoroughly heated. Uncover and bake an additional 5 minutes. Yield: 7 servings (serving size: 2 stuffed pasta shells and about ⅓ cup pasta sauce).

prep: 20 minutes • **cook:** 1 hour • **other:** 15 minutes

THREE CHEESE–CHERRY TOMATO LASAGNA

Available year-round with consistent quality, cherry tomatoes lend clean, bright flavor to this meatless, garden-fresh lasagna. As this dish bakes, the pasta cooks in the juice from the tomatoes.

1 cup (4 ounces) shredded part-skim mozzarella cheese
1 cup fat-free cottage cheese
¼ cup grated Parmesan cheese
1 teaspoon dried basil
½ teaspoon dried oregano
¼ teaspoon black pepper
½ teaspoon salt, divided
2 pints cherry tomatoes, halved
2 tablespoons olive oil
½ teaspoon crushed red pepper
¼ cup water, divided
Cooking spray
½ (8-ounce) package precooked no-boil lasagna noodles (6 noodles)
¼ cup chopped fresh basil

POINTS value:
7

exchanges:
2 starch
2 high-fat meat

per serving:
Calories 341
Fat 14.7g (saturated fat 5.4g)
Protein 21.3g
Carbohydrate 30.2g
Fiber 3.2g
Cholesterol 22mg
Iron 0.9mg
Sodium 714mg
Calcium 330mg

1. Preheat oven to 375°.
2. Combine first 6 ingredients and ¼ teaspoon salt in a bowl; stir well. Combine remaining ¼ teaspoon salt, cherry tomatoes, oil, and crushed red pepper in another bowl; toss gently to coat.
3. Pour 2 tablespoons water in an 8-inch square baking dish coated with cooking spray. Arrange 2 noodles over water. Spoon half of cheese mixture over noodles, spreading evenly. Top with one-third of tomato mixture. Repeat layers with another 2 noodles, remaining cheese mixture, and one-third of tomato mixture. Top with remaining 2 noodles and remaining tomato mixture. Drizzle with remaining 2 tablespoons water.
4. Cover tightly with foil, and bake at 375° for 1 hour. Let stand 15 minutes to allow pasta time to absorb juices from tomatoes. Sprinkle with basil; cut into 4 equal portions. Yield: 4 servings.

prep: 18 minutes • **cook:** 40 minutes • **other:** 5 minutes

Spinach–Artichoke Lasagna

Convenient ingredients are quickly stirred together and layered with no-boil noodles to create a satisfying meatless one-dish meal that's perfect for any busy weeknight menu.

POINTS value:
7

exchanges:
1½ starch
3 vegetable
2 medium-fat meat

per serving:
Calories 338
Fat 12.8g (saturated fat 6.9g)
Protein 21.7g
Carbohydrate 35.8g
Fiber 3.3g
Cholesterol 74mg
Iron 2.3mg
Sodium 874mg
Calcium 444mg

3   tablespoons grated Parmesan cheese, divided
2   tablespoons chopped fresh basil
1   teaspoon bottled minced garlic
1   (15-ounce) container part-skim ricotta cheese
1   (14-ounce) can artichoke hearts, drained and coarsely chopped
1   (10-ounce) package frozen chopped spinach, thawed, drained, and squeezed dry
1   large egg, lightly beaten
½   cup (2 ounces) shredded part-skim mozzarella cheese
½   cup (2 ounces) shredded sharp provolone cheese
1   (25.5-ounce) jar Italian herb pasta sauce (such as Muir Glen Organic)
Cooking spray
½   (8-ounce) package precooked no-boil lasagna noodles (6 noodles)

1. Preheat oven to 350°.
2. Combine 2 tablespoons Parmesan cheese and next 6 ingredients in a bowl; stir well. Combine mozzarella cheese and provolone cheese in a small bowl; toss well.
3. Spread ⅓ cup pasta sauce in bottom of an 8-inch square baking dish coated with cooking spray. Arrange 2 noodles over sauce; top with half of spinach mixture, ½ cup shredded cheese mixture, and ¾ cup pasta sauce. Arrange 2 noodles over sauce, and top with remaining spinach mixture and ¾ cup pasta sauce. Top with remaining 2 noodles; spread remaining pasta sauce over noodles.
4. Cover tightly with foil; bake at 350° for 30 minutes. Uncover; sprinkle with remaining ½ cup shredded cheese mixture and remaining 1 tablespoon Parmesan cheese. Bake, uncovered, an additional 10 minutes or until cheese melts. Let stand 5 minutes before serving. Cut into 6 equal portions. Yield: 6 servings.

PESTO LASAGNA WITH BOLOGNESE AND GARLIC CREAM

pictured on page 4

2 cups basil leaves
4 large garlic cloves, peeled and halved
2 tablespoons extravirgin olive oil
⅓ cup shredded Asiago cheese
2 tablespoons butter
6 large garlic cloves, minced
2½ tablespoons all-purpose flour
2 cups 1% low-fat milk
¾ teaspoon salt
½ teaspoon black pepper
6 cups Bolognese Sauce (see page 124)
Cooking spray
1 (8-ounce) package precooked no-boil lasagna noodles (12 noodles)

POINTS value:
8

exchanges:
1½ starch
2 vegetable
3 medium-fat meat

per serving:
Calories 377
Fat 15.2g (saturated fat 5.6g)
Protein 27.2g
Carbohydrate 32.9g
Fiber 3g
Cholesterol 64mg
Iron 2.3mg
Sodium 547mg
Calcium 177mg

1. Preheat oven to 350°.

2. Combine basil and 4 garlic cloves in a food processor; process until finely chopped. With processor on, slowly pour oil through food chute; process until well blended. Add Asiago; pulse 2 to 3 times until blended. Set pesto aside.

3. Melt butter in a medium saucepan over medium heat. Add minced garlic; sauté 1 minute. Add flour, and cook 2 minutes, stirring constantly with a whisk. Gradually add milk, stirring with a whisk until blended. Cook 6 minutes or until slightly thick, stirring constantly with a whisk. Remove from heat. Stir in salt and pepper.

4. Spread 1 cup Bolognese Sauce in bottom of a 13 x 9–inch baking dish coated with cooking spray. Top with 4 noodles; spread about 2 tablespoons pesto over noodles. Spread 2 cups Bolognese Sauce over pesto; drizzle with ½ cup white sauce. Repeat layers; top with remaining 4 noodles. Top with remaining pesto, Bolognese sauce, and white sauce.

5. Cover tightly with foil; bake at 350° for 1 hour or until thoroughly heated and noodles are tender. Let stand 5 minutes. Cut into 8 equal portions. Yield: 8 servings.

BOLOGNESE SAUCE

Spoon this delicious sauce over polenta or pasta, or use it in lasagna (see page 123). We reduced the amount of chopping by using prechopped vegetables sold in tubs in the produce department of large supermarkets.

POINTS value:
2

exchanges:
1 vegetable
2 very lean meat

per serving:
Calories 104
Fat 4.3g (saturated fat 1.4g)
Protein 13.1g
Carbohydrate 3.8g
Fiber 0.9g
Cholesterol 33mg
Iron 1.1mg
Sodium 177mg
Calcium 22mg

There are many variations of **Bolognese** (baw-law-NYEH-seh), but it's basically a thick sauce made with meat and vegetables and enhanced with wine and milk.

1	pound ground round
½	pound ground turkey (white and dark meat)
2	teaspoons olive oil
1	ounce pancetta or bacon, chopped (about ⅓ cup)
¼	cup chopped onion (about ½ small)
¼	cup chopped celery (about ½ stalk)
¼	cup chopped carrot (about 1 small)
1	teaspoon minced garlic
1	cup fat-free, less-sodium chicken broth
⅔	cup dry white wine or fat-free, less-sodium chicken broth
2	tablespoons tomato paste
1	(14.5-ounce) can petite-cut diced tomatoes, undrained
½	teaspoon black pepper
½	cup 2% reduced-fat milk
¼	teaspoon ground nutmeg

1. Cook ground round and turkey in a large nonstick skillet over medium-high heat until browned, stirring to crumble. Drain in a colander.

2. Heat olive oil in pan over medium-high heat. Add pancetta, and sauté 1 minute. Add onion and next 3 ingredients, and sauté 2 minutes or until vegetables are tender.

3. Return meat to pan. Add broth, wine, and tomato paste. Bring to a boil, and cook 5 minutes, stirring frequently. Add tomatoes and pepper; return to a boil. Reduce heat, and simmer, uncovered, 10 minutes. Stir in milk and nutmeg; cook 2 minutes or until thoroughly heated. Yield: 6 cups (serving size: ½ cup).

ARTICHOKE PESTO

Try this tangy sauce tossed with hot cooked pasta, served over fish or chicken, spread on baguette slices to make crostini, or as a refreshing dip with carrots and sliced cucumbers.

2	(14-ounce) cans quartered artichoke hearts, rinsed and drained
½	cup grated fresh Parmigiano-Reggiano cheese
¼	cup finely chopped fresh parsley
2	teaspoons grated fresh lemon rind
1	tablespoon fresh lemon juice
1	tablespoon olive oil
¼	teaspoon salt

1. Place artichokes in a food processor; pulse 5 times or until finely chopped. Add cheese and remaining ingredients; pulse to combine. Yield: 2¼ cups (serving size: ¼ cup).

POINTS value:
1

exchanges:
1½ vegetable
½ fat

per serving:
Calories 62
Fat 2.8g (saturated fat 1g)
Protein 3.7g
Carbohydrate 6.2g
Fiber 2g
Cholesterol 4mg
Iron 0.2mg
Sodium 459mg
Calcium 52mg

CHUNKY MARINARA SAUCE

This versatile sauce is perfectly suited to top your favorite pasta, but don't stop there. Use it to flavor fish or chicken for a quick entrée. It's an ideal sauce for spaghetti and meatballs, too. Or simply simmer some turkey Italian sausage in the sauce and serve the sausage hoagie-style. The sauce freezes well and can be ready in minutes with a quick thaw in the microwave. Microwave at MEDIUM-LOW (30% power) for 8 to 10 minutes, stirring occasionally.

POINTS value:
1

exchanges:
1 vegetable
½ fat

per serving:
Calories 57
Fat 2.4g (saturated fat 0.3g)
Protein 1.2g
Carbohydrate 6g
Fiber 1.2g
Cholesterol 0mg
Iron 0.5mg
Sodium 321mg
Calcium 5mg

2	(28-ounce) cans Italian-style plum tomatoes (such as Cento), undrained
1	tablespoon olive oil
½	cup chopped onion (½ small)
1	tablespoon minced garlic
1½	teaspoons salt
1	teaspoon sugar
4	teaspoons balsamic vinegar
¼	teaspoon freshly ground black pepper
¼	teaspoon crushed red pepper
1	large basil sprig
1	oregano sprig
1	bay leaf
2	tablespoons chopped fresh basil
1	tablespoon chopped fresh oregano

1. Place 1 can tomatoes with juice in a food processor, and process until smooth. Chop remaining can of tomatoes with juice.

2. Heat oil in a Dutch oven over medium-high heat. Add onion and garlic; sauté 3 minutes or until onion is tender. Add puréed tomatoes, chopped tomatoes with juice, salt, and next 7 ingredients. Bring to a boil; reduce heat, and simmer, uncovered, 20 minutes or until thick. Remove from heat; discard basil and oregano sprigs and bay leaf. Stir in chopped basil and chopped oregano. Yield: 6 cups (serving size: ½ cup).

MARGHERITA SAUCE

The classic Italian combo of tomatoes, basil, and cheese is typically found atop pizza, but the components shine in a minimally cooked sauce that's perfect for ladling over pasta, topping a chicken breast, or even filling an egg-white omelet.

2	teaspoons olive oil
2	tablespoons thinly sliced shallot (about 1 medium)
2	garlic cloves, minced
1	(28-ounce) can petite-cut diced tomatoes, drained
⅓	cup torn fresh basil leaves (about 12 leaves)
¼	teaspoon crushed red pepper
¼	teaspoon dried oregano
2	teaspoons balsamic vinegar
1	tablespoon grated fresh Parmigiano-Reggiano cheese

1. Heat oil in a large saucepan over medium-high heat. Add shallot and garlic; sauté 1 minute or until tender. Add tomatoes and next 3 ingredients; cook 3 minutes or until thoroughly heated. Remove from heat; stir in vinegar and cheese. Yield: 3 cups (serving size: ½ cup).

POINTS value:
1

exchanges:
1 vegetable
½ fat

per serving:
Calories 39
Fat 1.8g (saturated fat 0.4g)
Protein 1.3g
Carbohydrate 5.4g
Fiber 1.1g
Cholesterol 1mg
Iron 0.4mg
Sodium 93mg
Calcium 24mg

PUTTANESCA SAUCE
pictured on page 115

This robust, spicy sauce is a chunky mixture of tomatoes, onions, capers, olives, anchovies, and garlic. The word *puttanesca* (poot-tah-NEHS-kah) comes from *puttana*, for ladies of the night. Legend has it that the ladies lured men to their houses with this intensely fragrant sauce. It's most often served over pasta, but it tastes terrific spooned over filet mignon, chicken, or salmon, or tossed with shrimp.

POINTS value:
2

exchanges:
2½ vegetable
1 fat

per serving:
Calories 112
Fat 5.7g (saturated fat 0.7g)
Protein 2.1g
Carbohydrate 12.8g
Fiber 2.4g
Cholesterol 2mg
Iron 1.5mg
Sodium 535mg
Calcium 56mg

1   tablespoon olive oil
2½   cups chopped onion (2 medium)
1   cup coarsely chopped pitted kalamata olives
3   tablespoons capers
2   tablespoons minced garlic (about 6 cloves)
4   canned anchovy fillets, minced
1   (28-ounce) can fire-roasted crushed tomatoes (such as Progresso), undrained
1   teaspoon dried herbes de Provence
½   teaspoon freshly ground black pepper
¼   teaspoon crushed red pepper

1. Heat oil in a large saucepan over medium–high heat. Add onion, and sauté 6 minutes. Add olives and next 3 ingredients, and sauté 2 minutes. Add tomatoes and remaining ingredients; bring to a boil. Reduce heat, and simmer, uncovered, 10 minutes, stirring occasionally. Yield: 3 cups (serving size: ½ cup).

Sides

prep: 27 minutes • **cook:** 36 minutes

OVEN-BRAISED ARTICHOKES WITH GARLIC

Pan-searing the artichoke halves before braising with lemon and garlic gives them added flavor and color. The halved artichokes are beautiful topped with a sprinkling of fresh Parmesan cheese and served alongside veal, lamb, or chicken.

POINTS value:
3

exchanges:
3 vegetable
1½ fat

per serving:
Calories 137
Fat 7.5g (saturated fat 1.2g)
Protein 4.9g
Carbohydrate 15.8g
Fiber 7g
Cholesterol 1mg
Iron 1.7mg
Sodium 294mg
Calcium 79mg

4   medium artichokes (about 3¼ pounds)
2   large lemons, halved and divided
2   tablespoons olive oil, divided
½   cup water
1   teaspoon bottled minced garlic
¼   teaspoon salt
⅛   teaspoon black pepper
4   teaspoons finely shredded fresh Parmesan cheese

1. Preheat oven to 375°.

2. Cut off stem of each artichoke to within 1 inch of base; peel stem. Remove bottom leaves and tough outer leaves, leaving tender heart and bottom. Trim tips of leaves to remove thorns. Cut each artichoke in half lengthwise. Remove fuzzy thistle from bottom of each half with a spoon. Immediately rub cut surfaces of artichokes with 1 lemon half.

3. Heat 1 tablespoon oil in a large ovenproof stainless-steel skillet over medium-high heat. Place half of artichoke halves in pan, cut sides down; cook 2 minutes or until cut sides are browned and crusty. Remove from pan; set aside. Repeat procedure with remaining 1 tablespoon oil and remaining artichoke halves. Arrange all artichoke halves in pan. Squeeze 2 lemon halves over artichokes; add ½ cup water and garlic to pan. Cover and bake at 375° for 30 minutes or until a leaf near the center of each artichoke pulls out easily.

4. Place artichokes on a serving platter, cut sides up. Pour any pan juices over artichokes; squeeze remaining lemon half over artichokes. Sprinkle with salt, pepper, and Parmesan cheese. Yield: 4 servings (serving size: 2 artichoke halves).

Sautéed Broccoli Rabe with Garlic and Lemon

Look in the produce department of large supermarkets for fresh, full bunches of broccoli rabe (pronounced "broccoli rob"). This green, leafy vegetable has flowers that look similar to broccoli florets, and it contains phytochemicals that may protect against cancer. Blanching the vegetable in boiling water before sautéing reduces its characteristic bitter flavor.

1½	pounds broccoli rabe (rapini)
3	quarts water
2	tablespoons soft whole wheat breadcrumbs, toasted
1	tablespoon grated fresh Parmesan cheese
2	teaspoons olive oil
4	garlic cloves, minced
½	teaspoon salt
½	teaspoon grated fresh lemon rind
1	tablespoon fresh lemon juice
¼	teaspoon freshly ground black pepper
¼	teaspoon crushed red pepper

1. Thinly slice leafy greens of broccoli rabe. Peel tough lower stalk, and coarsely chop.

2. Bring 3 quarts water to a boil in a large Dutch oven. Add broccoli rabe, and cook 1 minute. Drain well; set aside. Combine breadcrumbs and cheese in a small bowl; stir well, and set aside.

3. Heat oil in a large nonstick skillet over medium-high heat. Add garlic, and sauté 30 seconds. Add broccoli rabe, and sauté 4 minutes or until tender. Add salt and next 4 ingredients; toss well. Place in a serving bowl; sprinkle with breadcrumb mixture. Serve immediately. Yield: 5 servings (serving size: 1 cup).

POINTS value:
2

exchanges:
1½ vegetable
½ fat

per serving:
Calories 69
Fat 2.2g (saturated fat 0.4g)
Protein 5.5g
Carbohydrate 8.3g
Fiber 0.2g
Cholesterol 1mg
Iron 1.3mg
Sodium 295mg
Calcium 82mg

Toasted Breadcrumbs: To make toasted soft breadcrumbs, place a slice of whole wheat bread in a food processor, and process until fine crumbs form. Spread the breadcrumbs on a baking sheet, and bake at 400° for 2 minutes or until toasted.

prep: 8 minutes • **cook:** 20 minutes

BRUSSELS SPROUTS WITH PANCETTA

Because a small amount of pancetta adds lots of flavor, you don't need to use much, which keeps down the fat and calories. Browning the butter gives the dish a nutty flavor; watch carefully, though, since butter can burn easily.

POINTS value:
2

exchanges:
1½ vegetable
1 fat

per serving:
Calories 83
Fat 5g (saturated fat 1.9g)
Protein 3.8g
Carbohydrate 7.9g
Fiber 2.8g
Cholesterol 8mg
Iron 1.3mg
Sodium 191mg
Calcium 40mg

1   quart water
1¼   pounds Brussels sprouts, trimmed and halved
¾   ounce thinly sliced pancetta
1   tablespoon butter
1½   tablespoons balsamic vinegar
¼   teaspoon salt
¼   teaspoon freshly ground black pepper
2   tablespoons chopped walnuts, toasted

1. Bring 1 quart water to a boil in a large nonstick skillet. Add Brussels sprouts, and boil 5 minutes or just until tender; drain well. Keep Brussels sprouts warm. Wipe pan dry with paper towels.
2. Cook pancetta in pan over medium-high heat until crisp. Remove pancetta from pan; drain on paper towels.
3. Melt butter in pan over medium heat; cook 2 minutes or until lightly browned, stirring occasionally. Add Brussels sprouts; stir in balsamic vinegar, salt, and pepper. Cook 3 minutes or until balsamic vinegar is slightly thick and mixture is thoroughly heated. Stir in pancetta. Remove from heat; sprinkle with toasted walnuts. Yield: 6 servings (serving size: ½ cup).

Italian Vegetable
Caponata, page 148

**Herbed Polenta with
Parmigiano-Reggiano, page 152**

Minted Peas with Prosciutto,
page 142

Charred Cauliflower

CHARRED CAULIFLOWER
pictured on facing page

Something magical happens when cauliflower is roasted to a crispy char: It gains an earthy sweetness that truffle-infused olive oil further enhances. For this recipe, we thought white truffle–infused oil was well worth the price, but we also loved it with lemon-infused and basil-infused oil, so feel free to substitute. Try Risi e Bisi on page 150 for another recipe that uses lemon-infused olive oil.

5   cups cauliflower florets (about 1 medium head or 1½ [12-ounce] packages)
1   tablespoon olive oil
½   teaspoon kosher salt
1   tablespoon fresh lemon juice
2   teaspoons white truffle–infused, lemon-infused, or basil-infused olive oil
¼   teaspoon crushed red pepper

1. Preheat oven to 500°.
2. Place cauliflower on a broiler pan. Drizzle with 1 tablespoon olive oil and salt; toss well to coat. Spread cauliflower in a single layer on pan. Bake at 500° for 15 minutes or until cauliflower is lightly browned in spots, stirring every 5 minutes.
3. Remove from oven. Drizzle charred cauliflower with lemon juice, 2 teaspoons infused oil, and crushed red pepper; toss well to coat. Yield: 4 servings (serving size: ¾ cup).

POINTS **value:**
1

exchanges:
1½ vegetable
1 fat

per serving:
Calories 82
Fat 5.8g (saturated fat 0.8g)
Protein 2.5g
Carbohydrate 7g
Fiber 3.2g
Cholesterol 0mg
Iron 0.6mg
Sodium 273mg
Calcium 28mg

EGGPLANT ROLLATINI

Bottled pasta sauce trims the time it takes to prepare this classic side dish. Be sure to cut the eggplant lengthwise to get flat, oblong slices that can be rolled around the cheese filling. This also makes an elegant vegetarian entrée with a **POINTS** value of 7 when you serve 3 rollatini per person.

POINTS value:
2

exchanges:
2 vegetable
1 medium-fat meat

per serving:
Calories 113
Fat 5.9g (saturated fat 2.9g)
Protein 7.3g
Carbohydrate 9.9g
Fiber 2.7g
Cholesterol 21mg
Iron 0.3mg
Sodium 291mg
Calcium 127mg

1   small eggplant (about 1 pound), trimmed and cut lengthwise into 6 (¼-inch-thick) slices
Cooking spray
¾   cup tomato-and-basil pasta sauce, divided
1   cup part-skim ricotta cheese
3   tablespoons grated Parmesan cheese
2   tablespoons chopped fresh basil
1   tablespoon pine nuts, toasted
⅛   teaspoon salt
1   small garlic clove, minced
3   tablespoons shredded part-skim mozzarella cheese

1. Preheat broiler.
2. Place eggplant slices on a baking sheet coated with cooking spray; lightly coat eggplant with cooking spray. Broil 5 minutes on each side or until browned and tender.
3. Reduce oven temperature to 400°.
4. Spread ¼ cup pasta sauce in bottom of an 8-inch square baking dish.
5. Combine ricotta cheese and next 5 ingredients in a bowl; stir well. Spoon 2 heaping tablespoons of ricotta mixture onto 1 end of each eggplant slice. Roll up slices, and place, seam sides down, in baking dish. Spoon remaining ½ cup pasta sauce evenly over rollatini, and sprinkle with mozzarella cheese. Bake at 400° for 35 minutes or until cheese is browned and bubbly. Yield: 6 servings (serving size: 1 rollatino).

BAKED FENNEL WITH ROASTED RED PEPPERS AND ASIAGO CHEESE

Fennel is one of the world's oldest known vegetables and is prized in Italian cooking. The simple preparation and the delicate yet distinctive flavor of aniseed make this dish a fitting partner for white fish.

2	quarts water
4	cups thinly sliced fennel bulb (about 2 medium bulbs)
1	cup thinly sliced bottled roasted red bell peppers
	Olive oil–flavored cooking spray
1	tablespoon butter, melted
¼	teaspoon salt
¼	teaspoon freshly ground black pepper
⅓	cup shredded Asiago cheese

1. Preheat oven to 400°.

2. Bring 2 quarts water to a boil in a large saucepan. Add fennel; cook 10 minutes or until tender. Drain.

3. Combine fennel and roasted red bell peppers in a 1½-quart casserole dish coated with cooking spray; toss well. Drizzle with melted butter, and sprinkle with salt and black pepper. Top with cheese. Bake at 400° for 17 minutes or until cheese is lightly browned. Yield: 4 servings (serving size: about 1 cup).

Note: To quickly slice fennel, use a food processor with a slicing attachment. To slice by hand, cut off the stalks, and cut the bulb in half from the top through the bottom. Place each half cut side down, and slice crosswise.

POINTS value:
2

exchanges:
2 vegetable
1 fat

per serving:
Calories 96
Fat 5.5g (saturated fat 3.4g)
Protein 3.7g
Carbohydrate 8.6g
Fiber 2.7g
Cholesterol 16mg
Iron 0.7mg
Sodium 391mg
Calcium 131mg

SAUCY MUSHROOMS

Select a variety of wild mushrooms for an earthy, full-flavored side that pairs well with roasted meats. We chose baby portobellos and chanterelles, but just about any wild variety you find in the store will work well in this recipe. Grated lemon rind and fresh lemon juice add a bright, tangy flavor to this rustic dish.

POINTS value:
1

exchanges:
1 vegetable
½ fat

per serving:
Calories 51
Fat 2.3g (saturated fat 0.3g)
Protein 2.4g
Carbohydrate 6.5g
Fiber 0.6g
Cholesterol 0mg
Iron 0.4mg
Sodium 273mg
Calcium 18mg

1 tablespoon olive oil
⅓ cup minced shallots (about 3 medium)
8 ounces whole baby portobello mushrooms
8 ounces chanterelle mushrooms
½ teaspoon salt
1 cup fat-free, less-sodium beef broth
1 teaspoon grated fresh lemon rind
3 tablespoons fresh lemon juice
1 tablespoon cornstarch
1 tablespoon minced fresh chives

1. Heat oil in a large nonstick skillet over medium–high heat. Add shallots; sauté 1 minute. Add mushrooms and salt. Reduce heat to medium, and cook 17 minutes or until moisture evaporates and mushrooms are tender, stirring frequently.
2. Combine beef broth and next 3 ingredients in a bowl, stirring with a whisk until well blended. Add to pan, and boil 1 minute or until slightly thick, stirring constantly. Remove from heat, and stir in chives. Yield: 6 servings (serving size: ½ cup).

prep: 14 minutes • **cook:** 25 minutes

ROMAN-STYLE SWEET-AND-SOUR ONIONS

Perfect for grilled meats and poultry, these onions are cooked down in a sweet balsamic vinegar–tomato sauce. Crisp bacon tops off the dish, adding a smoky undertone. Small, sweet *cipollini* ("little onions") are traditionally used, but we substituted coarsely chopped white onions. (See page 149 for more information on cipollini.)

2	center-cut bacon slices, coarsely chopped
4	medium white onions (about 1½ pounds), quartered and cut crosswise into thirds
⅓	cup orange juice
¼	cup balsamic vinegar
2	tablespoons tomato paste
1	tablespoon brown sugar
1	teaspoon fresh thyme leaves
½	teaspoon salt
¼	teaspoon freshly ground black pepper

1. Cook bacon in a large nonstick skillet over medium-high heat until crisp. Remove bacon from pan, reserving 1 teaspoon drippings in pan.

2. Place pan over medium-high heat. Add onion; sauté 18 minutes or until very tender and browned. Remove onion from pan; keep warm.

3. Add orange juice and next 6 ingredients to pan; stir well. Bring to a boil over medium-high heat, and cook 1 minute. Return onion to pan; cook 1 minute or until thoroughly heated. Remove from heat; sprinkle with bacon. Serve warm or at room temperature. Yield: 5 servings (serving size: ½ cup).

***POINTS* value:**
1

exchanges:
3 vegetable

per serving:
Calories 77
Fat 1g (saturated fat 0.4g)
Protein 2g
Carbohydrate 15.8g
Fiber 1.7g
Cholesterol 2mg
Iron 0.5mg
Sodium 295mg
Calcium 28mg

MINTED PEAS WITH PROSCIUTTO
pictured on page 135

The combination of salty prosciutto and sweet baby peas with a touch of mint is magical—proof that a simple serving of peas can have a powerful punch of flavor.

POINTS value:
1

exchange:
1 starch

per serving:
Calories 81
Fat 1.2g (saturated fat 0.4g)
Protein 6.4g
Carbohydrate 11.7g
Fiber 3.4g
Cholesterol 6mg
Iron 1.3mg
Sodium 307mg
Calcium 22mg

Cooking spray
2   ounces thinly sliced prosciutto, coarsely chopped (about ½ cup)
¼   cup finely chopped onion (½ small)
2   garlic cloves, minced
1   (16-ounce) package frozen petite green peas
⅓   cup fat-free, less-sodium chicken broth
1   tablespoon chopped fresh mint
¼   teaspoon grated fresh lemon rind
2   teaspoons fresh lemon juice
¼   teaspoon freshly ground black pepper
⅛   teaspoon salt

1. Heat a large nonstick skillet over medium-high heat. Coat pan with cooking spray. Add prosciutto, and cook 3 minutes, stirring frequently. Add onion and garlic; sauté 2 minutes or until tender.

2. Add peas and broth; cook 4 minutes or until peas are thoroughly heated. Remove from heat; stir in mint and remaining ingredients. Yield: 6 servings (serving size: ½ cup).

prep: 8 minutes • **cook:** 23 minutes

SMASHED PARMESAN POTATOES

Olive oil and premium Parmigiano-Reggiano cheese combine to add richness
and flavor to these coarsely mashed potatoes.

1½	pounds small red potatoes (about 9 potatoes)
⅔	cup fat-free milk
2	tablespoons extravirgin olive oil or butter
¼	cup shredded fresh Parmigiano-Reggiano cheese
½	teaspoon salt
½	teaspoon freshly ground black pepper

1. Place potatoes in a large saucepan, and cover with water; bring to a boil. Cover, reduce heat, and simmer 15 minutes or until potatoes are tender.

2. Drain potatoes well; return to pan. Add milk and olive oil to hot potatoes, and coarsely mash. Fold in cheese, salt, and pepper. Yield: 6 servings (serving size: about ⅔ cup).

Note: Add just enough water to cover the potatoes. Any more will only lengthen the time it takes to bring the water to a boil, therefore increasing your cook time.

POINTS **value:**
3

exchanges:
1½ starch
1 fat

per serving:
Calories 167
Fat 5.8g (saturated fat 1.3g)
Protein 4.8g
Carbohydrate 23.8g
Fiber 2.1g
Cholesterol 3mg
Iron 0.9mg
Sodium 271mg
Calcium 87mg

MINT AND GARLIC–ROASTED POTATOES

Mint may not be the first herb you would choose to pair with potatoes and garlic, but the flavor combination is outstanding. These potatoes are an ideal side for lamb, but they also pair well with roasted chicken.

POINTS value:
2

exchanges:
1 starch
½ fat

per serving:
Calories 103
Fat 2.4g (saturated fat 0.3g)
Protein 2.2g
Carbohydrate 18.4g
Fiber 2g
Cholesterol 0mg
Iron 0.9mg
Sodium 153mg
Calcium 15mg

2 pounds small red potatoes, quartered (about 13)
4 teaspoons olive oil, divided
½ teaspoon salt, divided
½ teaspoon freshly ground black pepper, divided
Cooking spray
¼ cup chopped fresh mint
1 garlic clove, minced

1. Preheat oven to 450°.
2. Combine potatoes, 1 teaspoon olive oil, ¼ teaspoon salt, and ¼ teaspoon pepper in a large bowl; toss well to coat potatoes. Arrange potatoes in a single layer on a jelly-roll pan coated with cooking spray. Bake at 450° for 30 minutes or until potatoes are tender and golden, stirring after 15 minutes.
3. Place potatoes in a large bowl. Add remaining 1 table-spoon olive oil, remaining ¼ teaspoon salt, remaining ¼ teaspoon pepper, mint, and garlic; toss well. Serve immediately. Yield: 8 servings (serving size: ¾ cup).

SAUTÉED SPINACH WITH RAISINS AND PINE NUTS

The combination of spinach, raisins, and pine nuts is commonly served in Genoa and the surrounding area along the Mediterranean. This nutritious side goes well with cooked meats (especially veal) and simply prepared fish. It's also a popular appetizer when served on crostini.

4	teaspoons pine nuts
1	teaspoon olive oil
2	garlic cloves, minced
2	(6-ounce) packages fresh baby spinach
¼	teaspoon salt
¼	teaspoon freshly ground black pepper
⅛	teaspoon crushed red pepper
	Dash of ground nutmeg
⅓	cup golden raisins

1. Place pine nuts in a large nonstick skillet over medium-high heat; cook 3 minutes or until lightly browned, stirring constantly. Remove from pan; set aside.

2. Heat oil in pan over medium-high heat. Add garlic; sauté 30 seconds. Add spinach; cook 4 minutes or until spinach wilts, stirring occasionally. Remove from heat; sprinkle with salt and next 3 ingredients. Add pine nuts and raisins; toss well. Serve immediately with a slotted spoon. Yield: 4 servings (serving size: ½ cup).

***POINTS* value:**
2

exchanges:
½ fruit
2 vegetable
½ fat

per serving:
Calories 104
Fat 3.2g (saturated fat 0.3g)
Protein 2.9g
Carbohydrate 19.6g
Fiber 4.7g
Cholesterol 0mg
Iron 3.1mg
Sodium 282mg
Calcium 70mg

ZUCCHINI AND COUSCOUS–STUFFED TOMATOES

You'll need only part of the prepared couscous for this recipe; save the rest to serve as a simple side dish another night. Enjoy these stuffed tomatoes with grilled chicken, lamb, or fish. Or serve two stuffed tomato halves per serving as a meatless main dish with a **POINTS** value of 5.

POINTS value:
2

exchanges:
1½ starch
1 vegetable

per serving:
Calories 133
Fat 1.4g (saturated fat 0.4g)
Protein 5.5g
Carbohydrate 26.5g
Fiber 2.6g
Cholesterol 1mg
Iron 0.8mg
Sodium 572mg
Calcium 47mg

1   (5.8-ounce) package roasted garlic–and–olive oil couscous (such as Near East)
Cooking spray
1   cup diced zucchini (1 medium)
½   cup chopped onion (½ small)
¼   cup chopped fresh basil
½   teaspoon salt, divided
¼   teaspoon freshly ground black pepper
2   large tomatoes (about 1¼ pounds)
4   teaspoons grated fresh Parmesan cheese

1. Preheat oven to 450°.
2. Prepare couscous mix according to package directions, omitting fat.
3. While couscous stands, heat a medium nonstick skillet over medium-high heat. Coat pan with cooking spray. Add zucchini and onion, and sauté 4 minutes or until tender. Remove from heat, and stir in basil, ¼ teaspoon salt, and pepper. Fluff couscous with a fork. Stir ¾ cup couscous into zucchini mixture; reserve remaining couscous for another use.
4. Cut tomatoes in half crosswise; remove and discard pulp and seeds from tomato halves. Place tomato halves in an 8-inch square baking dish, and sprinkle evenly with remaining ¼ teaspoon salt. Spoon zucchini mixture evenly into tomato halves. Sprinkle each stuffed tomato half with 1 teaspoon cheese.
5. Bake at 450° for 15 minutes or until tomatoes are soft and filling is thoroughly heated. Yield: 4 servings (serving size: 1 stuffed tomato half).

GRILLED ZUCCHINI WITH MINT AND OREGANO

It's not unusual when a rich chocolate dessert gets top ratings at our taste-testing table. But when a vegetable receives our highest score, you can rest assured that it's one tasty side dish. And this recipe did just that, so put this one on your "must try" list.

2	tablespoons olive oil
1	tablespoon balsamic vinegar
1	tablespoon red wine vinegar
½	teaspoon salt
½	teaspoon freshly ground black pepper
3	garlic cloves, minced
¼	cup chopped fresh mint, divided
¼	cup chopped fresh oregano, divided
6	zucchini (about 1¾ pounds), cut diagonally into ½-inch slices

1. Prepare grill.

2. Combine first 6 ingredients in a large bowl, stirring well with a whisk. Add 3 tablespoons mint and 3 tablespoons oregano.

3. Add zucchini slices, tossing gently to coat. Let stand at room temperature at least 15 minutes, stirring occasionally.

4. Remove zucchini from bowl, reserving marinade. Place zucchini slices on grill rack; cover and grill 3 minutes on each side or just until tender. Arrange zucchini on a platter; drizzle with reserved marinade, and sprinkle with remaining 1 tablespoon each of mint and oregano. Serve warm or at room temperature. Yield: 7 servings (serving size: about ½ cup).

POINTS value:
1

exchanges:
1 vegetable
1 fat

per serving:
Calories 59
Fat 4.2g (saturated fat 0.6g)
Protein 1.6g
Carbohydrate 5.1g
Fiber 1.4g
Cholesterol 0mg
Iron 0.5mg
Sodium 179mg
Calcium 34mg

ITALIAN VEGETABLE CAPONATA
pictured on page 133

The salty, acidic flavors of vinegar, tomatoes, capers, and kalamata olives harmonize with brown sugar and sweet raisins, creating a sweet-and-sour taste that's often found in Sicilian cooking.

POINTS value:
1

exchanges:
3 vegetable

per serving:
Calories 83
Fat 2.5g (saturated fat 0.3g)
Protein 2g
Carbohydrate 15.3g
Fiber 4.6g
Cholesterol 0mg
Iron 0.8mg
Sodium 316mg
Calcium 42mg

> **Caponata** (kap-oh-NAH-tah) is an eggplant-based dish that can be served alongside chicken, pork, or fish, or as an antipasto or condiment. Though most often served at room temperature, it's also good served warm or chilled.

1	large fennel bulb with stalks (about 1 pound)
1	tablespoon olive oil
1	large eggplant (about 1½ pounds), cubed
1	cup cubed zucchini (about 1 small)
½	cup chopped celery (1 stalk)
½	cup chopped onion (½ small)
4	garlic cloves, minced
1	(14½-ounce) can petite-cut diced tomatoes, undrained
⅓	cup golden raisins
¼	cup coarsely chopped pitted kalamata olives
1	tablespoon light brown sugar
1	teaspoon capers, coarsely chopped
¾	teaspoon salt
¼	teaspoon freshly ground black pepper
1	tablespoon balsamic vinegar

1. Remove and discard fennel stalks. Trim tough outer leaves from fennel bulb. Cut bulb in half through base. Cut out small pyramid-shaped core from each half; discard. Place cored fennel cut sides down; slice crosswise into 4 thick slices. Cut slices into cubes. Set aside.
2. Heat oil in a Dutch oven over medium-high heat. Add fennel, eggplant, and next 4 ingredients; sauté 10 minutes. Add tomatoes and next 6 ingredients; bring to a boil. Cover, reduce heat, and simmer 15 minutes, stirring occasionally. Uncover and cook 13 minutes or until most of liquid evaporates. Remove from heat; stir in balsamic vinegar. Yield: 10 servings (serving size: ½ cup).

prep: 17 minutes • **cook:** 49 minutes

HERB-ROASTED ROOT VEGETABLES

Little onions, baby carrots, and small red potatoes are fit for a king when roasted with fresh herbs and olive oil. A touch of balsamic vinegar adds sweetness to these earthy roots.

12   cipollini onions (about ½ pound)
1   pound baby carrots
6   small red potatoes (¾ pound), quartered
1   tablespoon fresh rosemary needles
1   teaspoon fresh thyme leaves
4   teaspoons olive oil
½   teaspoon kosher salt
½   teaspoon freshly ground black pepper
2   tablespoons chopped fresh flat-leaf parsley
1   tablespoon balsamic vinegar

POINTS value:
2

exchanges:
1 starch
2 vegetable

per serving:
Calories 130
Fat 3.2g (saturated fat 0.4g)
Protein 2.6g
Carbohydrate 23.1g
Fiber 3.4g
Cholesterol 0mg
Iron 0.6mg
Sodium 204mg
Calcium 35mg

1. Preheat oven to 475°.

2. Place onions in a medium saucepan, and cover with water. Bring to a boil, and cook 1 minute. Drain and plunge onions into ice water. Drain and peel.

3. Place onions, carrots, and potatoes in a broiler pan. Add rosemary and next 4 ingredients; toss to coat. Bake at 475° for 35 minutes, stirring after 17 minutes.

4. Place vegetables in a serving bowl. Add flat-leaf parsley and balsamic vinegar; toss gently. Yield: 6 servings (serving size: ¾ cup).

Cipollini: We found *cipollini* ("little onions") in a variety of supermarkets as well as specialty stores. They are small, round, flat onions that have a touch of sweetness. We also tested with two small Vidalia onions, chopped, and liked the flavor as well. To easily remove the skins from cipollini onions, boil them 1 minute, and then plunge them into an ice-water bath. The skins will slip off easily.

Risi e Bisi

This rice dish is similar to risotto, but it has a little more liquid and requires a lot less attention. You may use fresh peas when available, but we tested this recipe with frozen green peas, which are available year-round. If you purchase lemon-infused oil for this recipe, be sure to use the oil to also make Charred Cauliflower on page 137.

POINTS value:
3

exchanges:
2 starch

per serving:
Calories 148
Fat 2.4g (saturated fat 0.7g)
Protein 6.4g
Carbohydrate 26.6g
Fiber 2.3g
Cholesterol 2mg
Iron 0.4mg
Sodium 494mg
Calcium 45mg

> ***Rise e Bisi*** *(REE-see eh BEE-see), or "rice and peas" is a classic Venetian dish served in spring when baby green peas have just been harvested.*

1	(32-ounce) container fat-free, less-sodium chicken broth
2	teaspoons regular olive oil or lemon-infused olive oil
1	medium onion, chopped
1	garlic clove, minced
1	cup Arborio rice
1	cup frozen petite green peas
¼	cup shredded Parmesan cheese
⅛	teaspoon salt
¼	teaspoon freshly ground black pepper

1. Bring broth to a boil in a large saucepan; reduce heat to a very low simmer.

2. Heat oil in a large nonstick skillet over medium-high heat. Add onion and garlic; sauté 3 minutes. Add rice; cook 2 minutes. Add about two-thirds of hot broth, and bring to a boil. Reduce heat, and simmer, uncovered, 15 minutes, stirring occasionally. Add remaining broth; simmer an additional 5 minutes or until rice is tender. Stir in peas, cheese, salt, and pepper. Yield: 7 servings (serving size: ½ cup).

RICE WITH BUTTER AND SAGE

Just as oregano and basil are the perfect partners for pasta, sage marries well with rice. We kept this side simple and straightforward by not adding cheese, but Parmesan is often stirred in just before serving. Add a bit if you wish.

3   cups water
¾   teaspoon salt
1½   cups uncooked long-grain rice
1½   tablespoons butter
¼   cup finely chopped fresh sage
1   garlic clove, minced
2   teaspoons white wine vinegar

1. Bring 3 cups water and salt to a boil in a large saucepan. Add rice; cover, reduce heat, and simmer 19 minutes or until rice is tender and liquid is absorbed. Remove from heat; let stand, covered, 5 minutes.
2. While rice stands, melt butter in a small skillet over medium heat. Add sage and garlic; sauté 1 to 2 minutes or until garlic is golden. Add garlic mixture and vinegar to rice; toss well. Yield: 8 servings (serving size: about ⅔ cup).

POINTS value:
3

exchanges:
2 starch

per serving:
Calories 147
Fat 2.4g (saturated fat 1.4g)
Protein 2.6g
Carbohydrate 28g
Fiber 0.5g
Cholesterol 6mg
Iron 1.5mg
Sodium 235mg
Calcium 17mg

HERBED POLENTA WITH PARMIGIANO–REGGIANO

pictured on page 134

Serve soft polenta just as you would mashed potatoes. Try it with meats, such as Osso Buco with Gremolata (see page 83), and hearty stews. Or spoon it into a bowl and top it with a favorite sauce, such as Bolognese (see page 124). Use medium- or fine-textured yellow cornmeal rather than stone-ground, and make sure it's not a mix (which contains flour, leavening, and salt) or self-rising cornmeal (which has leavening and salt).

POINTS value:
3

exchanges:
1 starch
½ high-fat meat

per serving:
Calories 141
Fat 4.2g (saturated fat 2.4g)
Protein 6.9g
Carbohydrate 18.6g
Fiber 1.8g
Cholesterol 11mg
Iron 1.3mg
Sodium 959mg
Calcium 160mg

1 (32-ounce) container fat-free, less-sodium chicken broth
1 tablespoon chopped fresh rosemary
1 tablespoon butter
½ teaspoon freshly ground black pepper
¼ teaspoon salt
1 cup yellow cornmeal
½ cup grated fresh Parmigiano-Reggiano cheese
¼ cup chopped fresh flat-leaf parsley
Flat-leaf parsley sprigs (optional)

1. Bring first 5 ingredients to a boil in a large saucepan over medium heat. Gradually add cornmeal, stirring constantly with a whisk. Cook 3 minutes or until thick and bubbly, stirring constantly. Remove from heat; stir in cheese and parsley. Spoon into individual bowls. Garnish with flat-leaf parsley sprigs, if desired. Yield: 6 servings (serving size: about ⅔ cup).

Classic Caprese, page 165

Green Bean Salad with Olives, Walnuts,
and Red-Pepper Dressing, page 162

Insalata di Frutti di Mare,
page 168

Tuscan Bean Salad, page 163

Salads, Soups
& Breads

SICILIAN ORANGE SALAD

This Sicilian winter salad is usually prepared with blood oranges. We tested with more readily available navel oranges, and the salad was terrific. Serve this salad with your favorite grilled fish.

POINTS value:
2

exchanges:
1½ fruit
½ fat

per serving:
Calories 112
Fat 3.9g (saturated fat 0.5g)
Protein 1.7g
Carbohydrate 20.4g
Fiber 4g
Cholesterol 0mg
Iron 0.4mg
Sodium 337mg
Calcium 75mg

4   small navel oranges (about 2¼ pounds)
½   small red onion, cut in half lengthwise and thinly sliced (about ½ cup)
½   cup coarsely chopped pitted Sicilian green olives
1   tablespoon chopped fresh flat-leaf parsley
1   teaspoon olive oil
¼   teaspoon freshly ground black pepper
⅛   teaspoon salt

1. Peel and section oranges over a bowl; squeeze membranes to extract juice. Set sections aside, reserving ½ cup juice. Discard membranes.
2. Combine orange sections, onion, olives, and parsley in a medium bowl. Combine reserved ½ cup juice, oil, pepper, and salt; stir well with a whisk. Pour over salad; toss gently. Cover and chill 3 hours. Yield: 4 servings (serving size: ¾ cup).

BITTER GREENS WITH BLOOD ORANGES AND HAZELNUTS

A blood orange tastes like it has been kissed by a raspberry—tart and sweet. Its ruby red–streaked flesh adds vibrant, dramatic color to this salad. Quickly toast the hazelnuts for this recipe in a skillet over medium-high heat. The toasted nuts and spicy, slightly bitter greens lend the perfect balance of flavors to this beautiful salad.

3	medium blood oranges or navel oranges (2¼ pounds)
1	tablespoon minced shallot (1 medium)
2	tablespoons sherry vinegar or white wine vinegar
1½	tablespoons extravirgin olive oil
1	tablespoon honey
2	teaspoons minced fresh thyme
½	teaspoon black pepper
¼	teaspoon salt
4	cups baby arugula or spinach
4	cups spring mix salad greens
2½	cups torn radicchio (about ½ head)
2	tablespoons finely chopped skinless hazelnuts, toasted

1. Peel and section oranges over a bowl; squeeze membranes to extract juice. Set sections aside; reserve ⅓ cup juice. Discard membranes.

2. Combine reserved ⅓ cup juice, shallot, and next 6 ingredients in a small bowl; stir well with a whisk.

3. Combine arugula, spring mix greens, and radicchio in a large bowl. Pour dressing over salad; toss gently to coat. Divide salad evenly among plates; top with orange sections, and sprinkle with hazelnuts. Yield: 4 servings (serving size: about 2 cups salad, about ¼ cup oranges, and 1½ teaspoons hazelnuts).

***POINTS* value:**
3

exchanges:
½ fruit
3 vegetable
1½ fat

per serving:
Calories 161
Fat 7.8g (saturated fat 1g)
Protein 3.2g
Carbohydrate 21.1g
Fiber 4.5g
Cholesterol 0mg
Iron 1.6mg
Sodium 172mg
Calcium 120mg

ROASTED BEET SALAD

The bold, slightly bitter flavors of lemon rind, olive oil, and Gorgonzola complement the earthy, mildly sweet flavor of the beets.

POINTS value:
1

exchanges:
2 vegetable
1 fat

per serving:
Calories 84
Fat 3.8g (saturated fat 0.8g)
Protein 2.9g
Carbohydrate 10.8g
Fiber 3.1g
Cholesterol 2mg
Iron 1mg
Sodium 208mg
Calcium 34mg

2   pounds fresh beets (about 5 medium)
2   teaspoons olive oil, divided
¼   teaspoon salt, divided
½   teaspoon freshly ground black pepper, divided
2   teaspoons white wine vinegar
2   tablespoons minced shallot (1 large)
1   tablespoon finely chopped fresh sage
½   teaspoon grated fresh lemon rind
2   tablespoons chopped walnuts, toasted
2   tablespoons crumbled Gorgonzola cheese

1. Preheat oven to 450°.

2. Trim roots and stems from beets. Peel beets, and cut into ½-inch pieces. Combine beets, 1 teaspoon oil, ⅛ teaspoon salt, and ¼ teaspoon pepper in a medium bowl; toss well. Spread beets in a shallow roasting pan, and bake at 450° for 40 minutes or until tender.

3. Place beets in a medium bowl. Add remaining 1 teaspoon olive oil, remaining ⅛ teaspoon salt, remaining ¼ teaspoon pepper, vinegar, and next 3 ingredients; toss well. Sprinkle with walnuts and cheese. Serve at room temperature. Yield: 6 servings (serving size: ½ cup).

ROASTED CAULIFLOWER SALAD WITH OLIVES

Instead of camouflaging cauliflower with a cheese sauce, enjoy the subtle sweetness and mellow flavor of roasted cauliflower. Toss it with a light vinaigrette and tangy kalamata olives, and you'll have a salad everybody loves.

1   large head cauliflower, cut into bite-sized florets
      (about 6½ cups)
Olive oil–flavored cooking spray
1   tablespoon white wine vinegar
1   tablespoon extravirgin olive oil
½   teaspoon salt
¼   teaspoon crushed red pepper
1   garlic clove, minced
⅓   cup finely chopped pitted kalamata olives
2   tablespoons coarsely chopped fresh parsley

1. Preheat oven to 450°.
2. Place cauliflower on a baking sheet coated with cooking spray; lightly coat cauliflower with cooking spray. Bake at 450° for 20 minutes or until tender and lightly browned, stirring after 10 minutes.
3. While cauliflower cooks, combine vinegar and next 4 ingredients in a large bowl; stir well with a whisk. Add cauliflower, olives, and parsley to dressing in bowl; toss gently to coat. Serve warm or at room temperature. Yield: 5 servings (serving size: about 1 cup).

POINTS value:
1

exchanges:
1½ vegetable
1 fat

per serving:
Calories 84
Fat 5.3g (saturated fat 0.7g)
Protein 2.8g
Carbohydrate 8.1g
Fiber 3.4g
Cholesterol 0mg
Iron 0.8mg
Sodium 418mg
Calcium 35mg

GREEN BEAN SALAD WITH OLIVES, WALNUTS, AND RED-PEPPER DRESSING

pictured on page 154

Emerald-colored green beans, vibrant red tomatoes, and purple kalamata olives create a salad that's as beautiful as it is delicious. Serve with grilled beef, chicken, or fish.

POINTS value:
3

exchanges:
3 vegetable
1½ fat

per serving:
Calories 137
Fat 8.4g (saturated fat 0.9g)
Protein 3.5g
Carbohydrate 14.5g
Fiber 3.6g
Cholesterol 0mg
Iron 1.3mg
Sodium 402mg
Calcium 42mg

¼ cup white wine vinegar
2 tablespoons sugar
½ cup sliced red onion (½ small)
1 pound fresh green beans, trimmed
½ cup drained bottled roasted red bell pepper
2 tablespoons lemon juice
1 tablespoon olive oil
1 teaspoon honey
½ teaspoon salt
1 garlic clove, peeled and halved
1 cup cherry or grape tomatoes, halved
¼ cup coarsely chopped walnuts, toasted
10 pitted kalamata olives

1. Bring vinegar and sugar to a simmer in a small saucepan. Remove from heat; add onion, tossing to coat. Set aside.
2. Steam green beans, covered, 6 minutes or until crisp-tender.
3. While green beans cook, place roasted red bell pepper and next 5 ingredients in a food processor; process until smooth. Drain onion; discard vinegar mixture.
4. Rinse green beans under cold water; drain well. Combine green beans, onion, tomatoes, walnuts, and olives in a large bowl. Add bell pepper dressing; toss gently to coat. Serve warm, at room temperature, or chilled. Yield: 5 servings (serving size: 1 cup).

Tuscan Bean Salad
pictured on page 156

Chickpeas, which are popular in southern Italy, and cannellini beans, which are preferred in northern Italy, come together to offer variety in texture and flavor. Chickpeas (garbanzo beans) are firm and lend an earthy, nutty flavor, while cannellini beans (white kidney beans) are mild, slightly sweet, and creamy. Add a quick vinaigrette, fresh herbs, and chopped vegetables for a tasty side salad that complements chicken or lamb.

2	teaspoons grated fresh lemon rind
3	tablespoons fresh lemon juice
2	tablespoons red wine vinegar
2	tablespoons olive oil
1	teaspoon honey
½	teaspoon salt
½	teaspoon freshly ground black pepper
2	canned anchovy fillets, minced
3	garlic cloves, minced
1	cup halved grape tomatoes
¾	cup chopped English cucumber (¼ medium)
½	cup chopped celery (1 stalk)
½	cup thinly sliced red onion (½ small)
¼	cup chopped fresh flat-leaf parsley
1	tablespoon chopped fresh sage
1	(19-ounce) can chickpeas (garbanzo beans), rinsed and drained
1	(19-ounce) can cannellini beans or other white beans, rinsed and drained

POINTS value:
2

exchanges:
1 starch
1 fat

per serving:
Calories 142
Fat 5.3g (saturated fat 0.7g)
Protein 7.5g
Carbohydrate 16.4g
Fiber 4.1g
Cholesterol 10mg
Iron 1.9mg
Sodium 789mg
Calcium 68mg

1. Combine first 9 ingredients in a small bowl; stir well with a whisk.
2. Combine tomatoes and next 7 ingredients in a large bowl. Add dressing; toss gently.
3. Cover and chill at least 8 hours, stirring occasionally. Yield: 8 servings (serving size: about ¾ cup).

WILTED RADICCHIO AND CHICKPEA SALAD

A quick sauté tames the bitter flavor of the radicchio. The combination of robust flavors in this warm salad pairs well with a variety of roasted or grilled meats, such as lamb, beef, and chicken.

POINTS value:
5

exchanges:
2 starch
1½ vegetable
1 fat

per serving:
Calories 239
Fat 7.1g (saturated fat 0.6g)
Protein 9.6g
Carbohydrate 36.7g
Fiber 7.9g
Cholesterol 3mg
Iron 3.5mg
Sodium 492mg
Calcium 99mg

1	tablespoon olive oil
¾	cup chopped red onion (½ small)
2	large garlic cloves, minced
2	teaspoons sugar
3	canned anchovy fillets
1½	cups chopped radicchio (1 medium head)
¼	cup white wine vinegar
¼	teaspoon salt
2	(16-ounce) cans chickpeas (garbanzo beans), rinsed and drained
2	tablespoons chopped fresh flat-leaf parsley

1. Heat oil in a large nonstick skillet over medium-high heat. Add onion and garlic; sauté 8 minutes or until golden. Add sugar and anchovies; cook 2 minutes, breaking up anchovies with a wooden spoon. Add radicchio, vinegar, and salt; sauté 3 minutes or until radicchio wilts. Remove from heat. Stir in chickpeas and parsley. Serve warm. Yield: 4 servings (serving size: 1 cup).

CLASSIC CAPRESE
pictured on page 153

This simple Italian salad is beautiful and fast to assemble. Its success depends wholly on using top-quality fresh ingredients. We used a combination of red and yellow tomatoes for added color. Make the salad extraspecial with heirloom tomatoes, when available. At first glance, one might think that the vinegar has been accidentally omitted; however, this salad traditionally has no vinegar at all. Serve with toasted baguette slices, if desired.

2	medium tomatoes, each cut into 6 slices
8	ounces fresh mozzarella cheese, cut into 12 slices
¾	cup fresh basil leaves
4	teaspoons extravirgin olive oil
½	teaspoon salt
½	teaspoon freshly ground black pepper

1. Arrange 3 tomato slices, 3 cheese slices, and 3 table-spoons basil leaves on each of 4 salad plates; drizzle each with 1 teaspoon oil, and sprinkle each with ⅛ teaspoon salt and ⅛ teaspoon pepper. Serve immediately. Yield: 4 servings.

POINTS **value:**
6

exchanges:
1 vegetable
1 high-fat meat
2 fat

per serving:
Calories 222
Fat 17.1g (saturated fat 8.8g)
Protein 10.9g
Carbohydrate 5.2g
Fiber 1.1g
Cholesterol 45mg
Iron 0.9mg
Sodium 379mg
Calcium 337mg

From the region of Campania, **insalata Caprese** (kah-PRE-zee) is "salad in the style of Capri," an island in that region.

PANZANELLA

Juicy vine-ripened summer tomatoes are a must for this salad. The ciabatta bread should be slightly stale, so look for "day-old" sales at your local bakery.

POINTS value:
3

exchanges:
1 starch
1½ fat

per serving:
Calories 153
Fat 7.6g (saturated fat 1.9g)
Protein 5.1g
Carbohydrate 17.4g
Fiber 1.5g
Cholesterol 5mg
Iron 1.2mg
Sodium 305mg
Calcium 79mg

Panzanella
(pahn-zah-NEHL-lah) is a Tuscan tomato-and-bread salad.

¼ cup balsamic vinegar
3 tablespoons olive oil
¼ teaspoon salt
¼ teaspoon freshly ground black pepper
¼ teaspoon crushed red pepper
3 garlic cloves, minced
4 cups chopped tomato (about 3 large)
1 cup chopped cucumber (about 1 small)
¾ cup (3 ounces) diced part-skim mozzarella cheese
½ cup thinly sliced fresh basil
3 tablespoons chopped pitted kalamata olives (about 12)
1 (8-ounce) loaf day-old ciabatta bread, cut into ½-inch cubes

1. Combine first 6 ingredients in a small bowl; stir well with a whisk.
2. Combine tomato and next 5 ingredients in a large bowl. Pour dressing over salad; toss gently. Let stand at least 10 minutes or until dressing soaks into bread. Yield: 10 servings (serving size: 1 cup).

BARLEY SALAD WITH ASPARAGUS AND ARUGULA
pictured on page 3

Check out this high-fiber barley-vegetable mix; it's a great side for grilled seafood or chicken. Increase the serving size to 1½ cups for an excellent meatless main-dish salad with a **POINTS** value of 6.

½	pound thin asparagus spears
2	cups water
1	cup uncooked quick-cooking barley
2	tablespoons olive oil
2	tablespoons red wine vinegar
2	tablespoons fresh lemon juice
1	teaspoon freshly ground black pepper
2	teaspoons Dijon mustard
½	teaspoon salt
1½	cups trimmed arugula or spinach
1½	cups halved grape tomatoes
½	cup chopped red onion
⅓	cup (2¼ ounces) small diced smoked part-skim mozzarella cheese

POINTS value:
4

exchanges:
1½ starch
1 vegetable
1 fat

per serving:
Calories 200
Fat 7.7g (saturated fat 2.1g)
Protein 7.9g
Carbohydrate 27.6g
Fiber 6.5g
Cholesterol 6mg
Iron 1.9mg
Sodium 290mg
Calcium 106mg

1. Snap off tough ends of asparagus; discard. Cut asparagus into 2-inch pieces.
2. Bring 2 cups water to a boil in a large nonstick skillet. Add asparagus; cook 1 minute or until bright green and crisp-tender. Drain and plunge into ice water; drain.
3. Cook barley according to package directions, omitting salt and fat.
4. While barley cooks, combine olive oil and next 5 ingredients in a small bowl; stir well with a whisk.
5. Drain barley. Rinse under cold water; drain. Combine asparagus, barley, arugula, and next 3 ingredients in a large bowl. Add dressing; toss gently to coat. Serve at room temperature or chilled. Yield: 6 servings (serving size: 1 cup).

INSALATA DI FRUTTI DI MARE

pictured on page 155

POINTS value:
6

exchanges:
1 starch
2 vegetable
3 lean meat

per serving:
Calories 293
Fat 7.7g (saturated fat 1.2g)
Protein 32.7g
Carbohydrate 24.1g
Fiber 5.2g
Cholesterol 176mg
Iron 3.7mg
Sodium 958mg
Calcium 177mg

Insalata di Frutti di Mare

(ihn-sah-LAH-tah dee FROO-tee dee MAH-reh) translated means seafood salad. It can be prepared with a variety of seafood, but we limited this version to crab and shrimp to keep it quick and easy.

½ cup fat-free mayonnaise
2 teaspoons Dijon mustard
1 garlic clove, minced
1 teaspoon fresh lemon juice
4 small red potatoes (about 6 ounces), quartered
8 ounces small green beans or haricots verts, trimmed
1 cup thinly sliced red onion, separated into rings
3 tablespoons red wine vinegar
1 pint grape or cherry tomatoes, halved
1 medium yellow bell pepper, seeded and cut into ½-inch pieces
2 tablespoons chopped fresh flat-leaf parsley
2 tablespoons chopped pitted kalamata olives
1 tablespoon basil-infused olive oil or extravirgin olive oil
¼ teaspoon salt
¼ teaspoon cracked black pepper
1 pound lump crabmeat, drained and shell pieces removed
8 ounces jumbo shrimp (about 12 shrimp), cooked and peeled
4 Bibb, Boston, or radicchio lettuce leaves

1. Combine first 4 ingredients in a small bowl. Cover; chill.
2. Cook potatoes in boiling water 10 minutes or until tender. Remove potatoes from water with a slotted spoon; set aside. Add green beans to boiling water; cook 3 minutes or until crisp-tender; drain. Rinse green beans under cold water; drain.
3. While potatoes and green beans cook, combine onion and vinegar in a bowl; toss well. Let stand 10 minutes. Drain onion; discard vinegar.
4. Combine potatoes, green beans, onion, tomatoes, and next 6 ingredients in a large bowl; toss gently to coat.
5. Arrange 2 cups vegetables, about 3 ounces crabmeat, and 3 shrimp on each of 4 plates. Spoon 2 tablespoons mayonnaise mixture into each lettuce leaf; place 1 leaf on each plate. Serve immediately with Italian breadsticks, if desired. Yield: 4 servings.

SEARED STEAK SALAD WITH ROASTED PEPPERS AND ARUGULA

3 tablespoons minced fresh basil
2½ tablespoons balsamic vinegar
1 tablespoon olive oil
1 tablespoon honey
2 teaspoons minced fresh oregano
2 teaspoons prepared mustard
4 garlic cloves, minced and divided
2 cups drained bottled roasted red bell peppers, cut into strips
2 (8-ounce) beef tenderloin steaks (1 inch thick), trimmed
¼ teaspoon salt
⅛ teaspoon freshly ground black pepper
Olive oil–flavored cooking spray
1 cup (1-inch) cubed French bread
1 (5-ounce) bag arugula or spinach

POINTS value:
6

exchanges:
½ starch
2 vegetable
2 medium-fat meat

per serving:
Calories 246
Fat 11g (saturated fat 3.1g)
Protein 19.9g
Carbohydrate 16.1g
Fiber 1g
Cholesterol 54mg
Iron 3.4mg
Sodium 517mg
Calcium 83mg

1. Preheat oven to 375°.
2. Combine first 6 ingredients in a small bowl; stir in 2 minced garlic cloves. Add bell pepper strips; toss well, and set aside.
3. Heat a medium nonstick skillet over medium-high heat. Sprinkle steaks evenly with salt and black pepper; coat steaks with cooking spray. Add steaks to pan; cook 6 minutes on each side or until medium-rare or desired degree of doneness. Remove from pan; let stand 10 minutes.
4. While steaks stand, combine bread cubes and remaining minced garlic; toss well. Spread bread cubes in a single layer on a baking sheet coated with cooking spray. Bake at 375° for 8 minutes or until golden brown.
5. While bread bakes, place about 1½ cups arugula on each of 4 plates. Cut steaks diagonally across grain into thin slices. Remove bell pepper from bowl with a slotted spoon, reserving marinade. Divide steak and bell pepper evenly among salads. Drizzle reserved marinade evenly over each salad; top each salad with ¼ cup croutons. Yield: 4 servings.

ROMAN EGG–DROP SOUP

Unlike the Asian soup with a similar name, this soup contains small specks of cooked egg rather than ribbons of egg. The eggs look like *straccetti,* or "little rags," which explains the actual Italian name of the soup, *stracciatella* (straht-chee-ah-TEHL-lah) *alla Romana.*

POINTS value:
1

exchange:
1 lean meat

per serving:
Calories 49
Fat 2.2g (saturated fat 0.8g)
Protein 6.2g
Carbohydrate 1.3g
Fiber 0g
Cholesterol 72mg
Iron 0.4mg
Sodium 668mg
Calcium 28mg

2   (32-ounce) containers fat-free, less-sodium chicken broth, divided
3   tablespoons grated fresh Parmesan cheese
1   tablespoon minced fresh flat-leaf parsley
3   large eggs
1   large egg white
¼   teaspoon black pepper
⅛   teaspoon salt
⅛   teaspoon ground nutmeg

1. Combine 1 cup broth, grated cheese, and next 3 ingredients in a medium bowl; stir with a whisk until eggs are lightly beaten.
2. Bring remaining broth to a boil in a Dutch oven over medium-high heat. Reduce heat to low; gradually pour egg mixture into broth, stirring constantly with whisk (the faster you stir, the finer the pieces of egg). Cook 3 minutes, stirring constantly. Remove from heat; stir in pepper, salt, and nutmeg. Serve immediately. Yield: 9 servings (serving size: 1 cup).

prep: 11 minutes • cook: 37 minutes

TUSCAN CABBAGE AND POLENTA SOUP

Once the polenta is added to this soup, it should be the consistency of oatmeal—perfect for warming body and soul on cold winter days. Leftovers will continue to thicken and may be thinned with additional water or broth. Slices of toasted crusty Italian bread usually accompany this soup.

2 teaspoons olive oil
8 cups chopped green cabbage (about 1 small head)
1 cup chopped onion (1 medium)
5 garlic cloves, minced
2 (32-ounce) containers fat-free, less-sodium chicken broth
½ teaspoon salt
¼ teaspoon black pepper
1 bay leaf
¾ cup instant dry polenta
6 tablespoons grated fresh Parmesan cheese

POINTS value:
2

exchanges:
½ starch
1 vegetable
1 lean meat

per serving:
Calories 108
Fat 2.1g (saturated fat 0.7g)
Protein 6.5g
Carbohydrate 14g
Fiber 3g
Cholesterol 3mg
Iron 0.5mg
Sodium 773mg
Calcium 73mg

1. Heat oil in a Dutch oven over medium heat. Add cabbage, onion, and garlic; cook 12 minutes or until almost tender. Add broth, salt, pepper, and bay leaf; bring to a boil. Reduce heat, and simmer, uncovered, 12 minutes or until cabbage is tender. Slowly add polenta, stirring constantly with a whisk. Simmer 5 minutes or until thick. Discard bay leaf. Ladle soup into individual bowls, and sprinkle with cheese. Yield: 9 servings (serving size: 1 cup soup and 2 teaspoons cheese).

CREAM OF ARTICHOKE SOUP

pictured on facing page

Whole milk adds richness to this soup in the same way half-and-half or cream would—but with significantly fewer calories and less fat.

POINTS value:
4

exchanges:
½ starch
3½ vegetable
1½ fat

per serving:
Calories 195
Fat 7.8g (saturated fat 4.4g)
Protein 7.8g
Carbohydrate 24.7g
Fiber 5.1g
Cholesterol 19mg
Iron 0.7mg
Sodium 604mg
Calcium 118mg

2	tablespoons butter
3	cups frozen country-style shredded hash brown potatoes (such as Ore-Ida)
2	cups frozen chopped onion
½	cup matchstick-cut carrot
2	teaspoons minced garlic
1	(9-ounce) package frozen artichoke hearts, thawed
3	cups fat-free, less-sodium chicken broth
½	teaspoon black pepper
¼	teaspoon salt
1	cup whole milk
2½	tablespoons chopped drained oil-packed sun-dried tomatoes
2½	tablespoons shredded fresh Parmigiano-Reggiano or Parmesan cheese

1. Melt butter in a large saucepan over medium-high heat. Add hash brown potatoes and next 4 ingredients; sauté 6 minutes or until vegetables are tender. Add broth, pepper, and salt, and bring to a boil. Cover, reduce heat, and simmer 20 minutes.

2. Place half of potato mixture in a blender, and process until smooth. Pour puréed soup into a bowl, and repeat procedure with remaining half of potato mixture. Return puréed soup to pan; stir in milk. Cook over medium-high heat 2 minutes or until thoroughly heated. Ladle soup into individual bowls; top with sun-dried tomatoes, and sprinkle with cheese. Serve immediately. Yield: 5 servings (serving size: 1¼ cups soup, 1½ teaspoons sun-dried tomatoes, and 1½ teaspoons cheese).

Cream of Artichoke Soup

Leek and Scallop Stew,
page 182

Lemon-Rosemary Focaccia,
page 188

Pasta e Fagioli, page 183

RIBOLLITA

It's rare to find a *trattoria* (neighborhood restaurant) in Tuscany that doesn't serve this soup. While most agree that the flavor improves after chilling the soup overnight, it's great when freshly made, too. The bread is often stirred into the soup as it cooks; here, each serving is topped with a slice of rustic bread and drizzled with extravirgin olive oil.

3   tablespoons extravirgin olive oil, divided
1   (10-ounce) package frozen seasoning blend with onion, celery, red and green bell pepper, and parsley (such as McKenzie's)
2   teaspoons bottled minced roasted garlic
1   (19-ounce) can cannellini beans or other white beans, rinsed, drained, and divided
7   cups thinly sliced fresh kale (about 13 ounces)
2   tablespoons sun-dried tomato paste or regular tomato paste
1   teaspoon dried thyme
¼   teaspoon salt
¼   teaspoon black pepper
1   (32-ounce) container fat-free, less-sodium chicken broth
1   (14.5-ounce) can diced tomatoes, undrained
8   (1-ounce) slices Italian bread (½ inch thick)

1. Heat 5 teaspoons oil in a Dutch oven over medium heat. Add seasoning blend and garlic; sauté 5 minutes or until vegetables are very tender. Add 1 cup beans, kale, and next 6 ingredients; bring to a boil. Reduce heat; simmer, uncovered, 30 minutes or until kale is tender, stirring occasionally.
2. While soup simmers, mash remaining beans in a small bowl using a potato masher.
3. Add mashed beans to soup; simmer 15 minutes or until slightly thick. Ladle soup into individual bowls; top with bread, and drizzle with remaining oil. Yield: 8 servings (serving size: 1 cup soup, 1 bread slice, and ½ teaspoon oil).

Note: If frozen seasoning blend is not available in your area, you may substitute ¾ cup each of finely chopped onion, celery, and red or green bell pepper, plus 2 tablespoons minced fresh parsley; sauté 8 minutes or until tender.

POINTS value:
4

exchanges:
1½ starch
2 vegetable
1 fat

per serving:
Calories 228
Fat 7g (saturated fat 1g)
Protein 8.5g
Carbohydrate 33.2g
Fiber 4.9g
Cholesterol 0mg
Iron 2.8mg
Sodium 728mg
Calcium 126mg

Ribollita (ree-boh-LEE-tah), or "reboiled" soup, is traditionally made a day ahead and then reheated before it's served.

TUSCAN CHICKPEA SOUP

Evoke the flavors of a Tuscan farmhouse kitchen with the satisfying combination of nutty beans, fresh herbs, and garlic. Any small pasta that you have on hand will work to add texture to this puréed soup. The pasta will continue to thicken the soup as it stands. Thin leftovers with additional water or broth.

POINTS value:
3

exchanges:
2 starch
½ fat

per serving:
Calories 182
Fat 4.1g (saturated fat 0.3g)
Protein 5.8g
Carbohydrate 30.4g
Fiber 4.5g
Cholesterol 0mg
Iron 1.9mg
Sodium 403mg
Calcium 41mg

½ cup uncooked ditalini (very short tube–shaped macaroni), acini di pepe (tiny round pasta), or orzo
1 tablespoon olive oil
1¼ cups chopped onion (1 large)
½ cup finely chopped carrot (about 2 carrots)
1 tablespoon minced garlic
1 tablespoon chopped fresh rosemary
2 teaspoons chopped fresh thyme
2½ cups vegetable broth (such as Swanson), divided
2 cups water
2 (15½-ounce) cans chickpeas (garbanzo beans), rinsed and drained
½ teaspoon freshly ground black pepper
¼ teaspoon salt

1. Cook pasta according to package directions, omitting salt and fat.

2. While pasta cooks, heat oil in a Dutch oven over medium-high heat. Add onion, carrot, and garlic; sauté 5 minutes or until vegetables are tender. Add rosemary and thyme; sauté 30 seconds. Add 1½ cups broth and water; bring to a boil. Reduce heat, and simmer, uncovered, 10 minutes.

3. Drain pasta; set aside.

4. Reserve ½ cup chickpeas; set aside. Place remaining chickpeas and remaining 1 cup broth in a blender; process 1 minute or until smooth. Pour puréed chickpea mixture into a large bowl. Place half of soup in blender; process until smooth. Pour puréed soup into bowl. Repeat procedure with remaining half of soup.

5. Return puréed soup to pan. Stir in reserved ½ cup chickpeas, pepper, and salt. Cook over medium heat 6 minutes or until thoroughly heated. Stir in cooked pasta. Serve immediately. Yield: 7 servings (serving size: 1 cup).

CHILLED FENNEL SOUP

The sweet start and peppery finish of this soup make it a refreshing first course of an alfresco summer meal. A small amount of half-and-half adds body and rich flavor to this smooth, creamy soup.

1	tablespoon butter
8	cups sliced fennel bulb (about 2 medium bulbs)
2	cups sliced sweet onion (about 1 large)
½	cup sweet white Italian wine (such as Moscato)
1	(32-ounce) container fat-free, less-sodium chicken broth
2	teaspoons chicken soup base (such as Better than Bouillon)
½	cup half-and-half
½	teaspoon freshly ground black pepper

Fennel fronds (optional)

1. Melt butter in a large Dutch oven over medium-high heat. Add sliced fennel and onion, and sauté 9 minutes or until lightly browned. Add wine, chicken broth, and soup base, and bring to a boil. Reduce heat, and simmer, uncovered, 30 minutes or until fennel is very tender. Remove from heat; cool 10 minutes.

2. Place half of fennel mixture in a blender or food processor; process until very smooth. Pour puréed soup into a large bowl; repeat procedure with remaining half of fennel mixture. Stir in half-and-half and pepper. Cover and refrigerate at least 3 hours or until thoroughly chilled. Ladle soup into individual bowls. Garnish with fennel fronds, if desired. Yield: 7 servings (serving size: 1 cup).

POINTS **value:**
1

exchanges:
2 vegetable
1 fat

per serving:
Calories 90
Fat 3.9g (saturated fat 2.3g)
Protein 4.1g
Carbohydrate 11.6g
Fiber 3.4g
Cholesterol 11mg
Iron 0.9mg
Sodium 609mg
Calcium 76mg

LEEK SOUP

A simple blend of caramelized leeks topped with a broth-soaked slice of cheese toast really hit the spot at our taste testing. *Parrano Originale* is a slightly sweet and nutty cheese that melts well and is not stringy. If this cheese is not available in your area, substitute Dutch Gouda or Swiss cheese.

POINTS value:
7

exchanges:
2 starch
3 vegetable
1 high-fat meat

per serving:
Calories 322
Fat 9.2g (saturated fat 5.1g)
Protein 14.7g
Carbohydrate 45.3g
Fiber 3.3g
Cholesterol 23mg
Iron 3.2mg
Sodium 1,119mg
Calcium 256mg

1	tablespoon butter
4	cups thinly sliced leek (about 4 large)
5	garlic cloves, minced
5	cups fat-free, less-sodium chicken broth
4	thyme sprigs
1	bay leaf
5	(½-inch-thick) slices diagonally cut French bread baguette
⅓	cup (1⅓ ounces) shredded Parrano Originale cheese

1. Melt butter in a large saucepan over medium heat. Add leek and garlic; sauté 15 minutes or until golden. Add broth, thyme, and bay leaf; bring to a boil. Reduce heat, and simmer, uncovered, 15 minutes.

2. While soup simmers, preheat boiler. Place baguette slices on a large baking sheet, and sprinkle evenly with cheese. Broil 4 minutes or until cheese melts and bread is toasted.

3. Remove soup from heat, and discard bay leaf. Ladle soup into individual bowls, and top with cheese toast. Yield: 5 servings (serving size: about 1 cup soup and 1 slice cheese toast).

SPINACH SOUP WITH HAZELNUTS

Make sure the hazelnuts are well-toasted for the best-tasting soup. Chopping the hazelnuts before they are blended insures a velvety, smooth purée. We found a blender works best for puréeing the soup.

½	cup hazelnuts
1	teaspoon olive oil
2	cups diced onion (1 large)
3	garlic cloves, minced
1	(32-ounce) container fat-free, less-sodium chicken broth, divided
1	(10-ounce) package frozen chopped spinach, thawed, drained, and squeezed dry
¼	teaspoon salt
¼	cup all-purpose flour
2	cups fat-free half-and-half
⅓	cup grated fresh Parmesan cheese
⅛	teaspoon freshly ground black pepper

POINTS value:
3

exchanges:
½ starch
2 vegetable
1½ fat

per serving:
Calories 160
Fat 7.8g (saturated fat 1.7g)
Protein 8.1g
Carbohydrate 16.5g
Fiber 2.6g
Cholesterol 6mg
Iron 1.4mg
Sodium 564mg
Calcium 171mg

1. Preheat oven to 350°.

2. Place nuts on a baking sheet. Bake at 350° for 15 minutes or until fragrant and browned, stirring once. Turn nuts out onto a towel. Roll up towel; rub off skins. Chop nuts.

3. While hazelnuts toast, heat olive oil in a Dutch oven over medium heat. Add onion and garlic; sauté 5 minutes or until golden. Add 3 cups broth, spinach, and salt; bring to a boil. Reduce heat, and simmer, uncovered, 10 minutes.

4. While soup simmers, combine chopped hazelnuts and remaining broth in a blender; process until very smooth. Add flour, and process until well blended. Add broth mixture to soup in pan, stirring with a whisk until blended. Simmer, uncovered, 5 minutes or until slightly thick, stirring occasionally. Remove from heat; stir in half-and-half, cheese, and pepper.

5. Place half of soup in blender; process until very smooth. Pour puréed soup into a bowl; repeat procedure with remaining half of soup. Return puréed soup to pan. Cook over medium heat 5 minutes or until thoroughly heated, stirring occasionally. Yield: 8 servings (serving size: 1 cup).

LEEK AND SCALLOP STEW
pictured on page 174

The keys to perfectly seared scallops are a very hot skillet and not overcrowding the pan. Simmer scallops in the stew only until they are done so that they remain tender. For an elegant presentation, set aside some of the sautéed leek to garnish each serving.

POINTS value:
4

exchanges:
3 vegetable
2 lean meat

per serving:
Calories 185
Fat 4.2g (saturated fat 1.4g)
Protein 21.7g
Carbohydrate 14.1g
Fiber 1.9g
Cholesterol 43mg
Iron 1.6mg
Sodium 737mg
Calcium 82mg

1   pound large sea scallops, cut in half horizontally (about 12 scallops)
Cooking spray
1   teaspoon olive oil
1   cup thinly sliced leek (1 large)
2   teaspoons bottled minced garlic
1   cup dry white wine or fat-free, less-sodium chicken broth
1   cup fat-free, less-sodium chicken broth
1½ teaspoons chopped fresh thyme
½   teaspoon salt
½   teaspoon black pepper
1   (14.5-ounce) can diced tomatoes, drained well
¼   cup half-and-half
¼   cup chopped fresh cilantro
2   tablespoons dry breadcrumbs
1   tablespoon grated fresh lemon rind

1. Pat scallops dry with a paper towel; lightly coat scallops with cooking spray. Heat a large nonstick skillet over medium-high heat. Add one-third of scallops; sear 2 minutes on each side or until lightly browned. Remove scallops from pan. Repeat procedure twice with remaining scallops.
2. While scallops cook, heat olive oil in a large saucepan coated with cooking spray over medium-high heat. Add leek and garlic; sauté 4 minutes or until tender. Add wine and next 5 ingredients; bring to a boil. Reduce heat, and simmer, uncovered, 5 minutes. Add scallops, and simmer 3 minutes. Remove from heat; stir in half-and-half.
3. Combine cilantro, breadcrumbs, and lemon rind in a small bowl; stir well. Ladle stew into individual bowls; top with breadcrumb mixture. Yield: 4 servings (serving size: 1¼ cups stew and about 2 tablespoons breadcrumb mixture).

PASTA E FAGIOLI
pictured on page 176

You'll have enough of this family favorite for a filling dinner plus lunch the next day. It makes fabulous leftovers and freezes well.

1	pound ground round
1	cup chopped onion (1 small)
¾	cup chopped celery (2 stalks)
¾	cup chopped carrot (2 medium)
2	garlic cloves, minced
1	(28-ounce) can fire-roasted crushed tomatoes, undrained
2	(14-ounce) cans fat-free, less-sodium beef broth
1	(16-ounce) can red kidney beans, rinsed and drained
1	(15-ounce) can cannellini beans or other white beans, rinsed and drained
1½	teaspoons dried Italian seasoning
½	teaspoon black pepper
¼	teaspoon salt
¼	teaspoon crushed red pepper
¾	cup uncooked ditalini (very short tube-shaped macaroni)
2	tablespoons grated fresh Parmesan cheese

1. Cook beef and next 4 ingredients in a Dutch oven over medium-high heat until beef is browned, stirring to crumble. Drain well, and return to pan.

2. Add tomatoes and next 7 ingredients; bring to a boil. Reduce heat, and simmer, uncovered, 15 minutes. Add ditalini; cook 15 minutes or until pasta is done. Ladle soup into individual bowls; sprinkle with cheese. Yield: 6 servings (serving size: 1½ cups soup and 1 teaspoon cheese).

POINTS **value:**
5

exchanges:
2 starch
2 vegetable
2 very lean meat

per serving:
Calories 297
Fat 4g (saturated fat 1.4g)
Protein 25.6g
Carbohydrate 39.1g
Fiber 8.3g
Cholesterol 41mg
Iron 4.7mg
Sodium 800mg
Calcium 109mg

> **Pasta e Fagioli** (fa-ZHOH-lee), or pasta-and-bean soup, is a complete meal all in itself.

Lentil Soup with Pancetta and Parmesan

Adding a few fresh ingredients to canned soup gives this soup a made-from-scratch flavor with very little time in the kitchen.

POINTS value:
3

exchanges:
1 starch
1 vegetable
1 fat

per serving:
Calories 152
Fat 4.4g (saturated fat 1.7g)
Protein 8.9g
Carbohydrate 19.2g
Fiber 2.8g
Cholesterol 8mg
Iron 1.8mg
Sodium 740mg
Calcium 63mg

¾ cup chopped onion (about 1 small)
2 ounces pancetta, diced (about ⅓ cup)
3 garlic cloves, minced
3 cups fat-free, less-sodium chicken broth, divided
½ cup water
2 (19-ounce) cans 99% fat-free lentil soup (such as Progresso)
1 bay leaf
¼ cup grated Parmesan cheese

1. Place first 3 ingredients in a large saucepan; cook over medium heat 9 minutes or until onion is golden. Add 1 cup broth, scraping pan to loosen browned bits. Stir in remaining 2 cups broth, water, soup, and bay leaf; bring to a boil. Reduce heat, and simmer, uncovered, 20 minutes. Discard bay leaf. Ladle soup into individual bowls; sprinkle with Parmesan cheese. Yield: 7 servings (serving size: 1 cup soup and about 1½ teaspoons cheese).

POTATO CHOWDER WITH PANCETTA AND ROSEMARY

This smoky herbed potato-leek chowder makes itself at home at just about any dinner table. Crispy bits of pancetta are a tasty treat in every bowl. Start the pancetta in a cold pan to prevent it from sticking, and stir often to evenly brown the pieces.

4   ounces pancetta, diced (about ⅔ cup)
2   cups diced leek (about 1 large)
2   garlic cloves, minced
8   cups (1-inch) cubed peeled baking potato (about 3 pounds)
4   cups fat-free, less-sodium chicken broth
¼   teaspoon salt
1   cup fat-free half-and-half
1   teaspoon finely chopped fresh rosemary
¼   teaspoon black pepper

1. Place pancetta in a Dutch oven, and cook over medium heat 4 minutes or until browned, stirring frequently. Add leek and garlic; sauté 1 minute. Add potato, broth, and salt; bring to a boil. Reduce heat, and simmer, uncovered, 26 minutes or until potato is very tender, stirring occasionally. Remove from heat; stir in remaining ingredients. Yield: 9 servings (serving size: 1 cup).

POINTS value:
4

exchanges:
2½ starch

per serving:
Calories 219
Fat 4.6g (saturated fat 2.1g)
Protein 7.1g
Carbohydrate 38.2g
Fiber 2.6g
Cholesterol 10mg
Iron 1mg
Sodium 904mg
Calcium 46mg

ESCAROLE SOUP

If you've never tried escarole, this comforting chicken-and-rice soup will make you fall in love with this mild, slightly bitter green vegetable. The quickest way to get chicken for this soup is to use a deli rotisserie chicken. Both breast halves should give you 2 cups of chopped meat, and you'll have the rest of the chicken for another meal.

POINTS value:
3

exchanges:
1 starch
2 very lean meat

per serving:
Calories 163
Fat 2.9g (saturated fat 0.6g)
Protein 16.9g
Carbohydrate 16.8g
Fiber 1.9g
Cholesterol 34mg
Iron 1.4mg
Sodium 613mg
Calcium 42mg

2   teaspoons olive oil
1   cup chopped onion (1 medium)
3   garlic cloves, minced
6   cups coarsely chopped packed escarole (about 5 ounces)
½   cup dry white wine or fat-free, less-sodium chicken broth
6   cups fat-free, less-sodium chicken broth
2   cups chopped roasted skinless, boneless chicken breast
½   cup uncooked long-grain rice
1   teaspoon fresh thyme leaves
¼   teaspoon salt
1   bay leaf

1. Heat oil in a Dutch oven over medium heat. Add onion and garlic; sauté 7 minutes or until tender and lightly browned. Add escarole; sauté 2 minutes or just until escarole wilts. Add wine; cook 1 minute. Add broth and remaining ingredients; bring to a boil. Cover, reduce heat, and simmer 20 minutes or until rice is tender. Discard bay leaf before serving. Yield: 7 servings (serving size: 1 cup).

ROSEMARY-PROSCIUTTO BREADSTICKS

No one will guess that these savory breadsticks are made with refrigerated breadstick dough when they're served hot from the oven.

1   (11-ounce) can refrigerated soft breadstick dough
1½   ounces thinly sliced prosciutto
Olive oil–flavored cooking spray
3   tablespoons grated Parmesan cheese
2   teaspoons minced fresh rosemary

1. Preheat oven to 375°.
2. Separate breadstick dough into 12 pieces; cut each piece in half lengthwise to form 2 thin strips. Wrap prosciutto around 12 dough strips. Twist unwrapped dough strips around prosciutto-wrapped pieces; twist 3 or 4 times, pinching ends to seal. Coat twists with cooking spray.
3. Combine cheese and rosemary in a pie plate or shallow dish; roll breadsticks in cheese mixture. Place breadsticks on a baking sheet coated with cooking spray. Bake at 375° for 13 minutes or until golden. Serve warm. Yield: 1 dozen (serving size: 1 breadstick).

POINTS value:
2

exchange:
1 starch

per serving:
Calories 85
Fat 2g (saturated fat 0.3g)
Protein 3.3g
Carbohydrate 12.7g
Fiber 0.4g
Cholesterol 3mg
Iron 0.8mg
Sodium 266mg
Calcium 15mg

LEMON–ROSEMARY FOCACCIA

pictured on page 175

We used refrigerated dinner roll dough as a shortcut to fresh-from-the-oven bread. Cooking on the lowest oven rack crisps the bottom of the bread, giving it a more traditional crunch.

POINTS value:
3

exchanges:
1 starch
1 fat

per serving:
Calories 111
Fat 5.3g (saturated fat 1.1g)
Protein 2.3g
Carbohydrate 13.1g
Fiber 0.3g
Cholesterol 0mg
Iron 0.9mg
Sodium 306mg
Calcium 3mg

Focaccia (foh-KAH-chee-ah) is a flat, slightly raised bread that is particularly popular in the coastal regions of Italy, where the humid air prevents full rising of traditional yeast dough.

---

1 (8-ounce) can refrigerated reduced-fat crescent dinner roll dough
1 small lemon, cut into paper-thin slices
1 tablespoon fresh rosemary leaves
1 tablespoon pine nuts
¼ teaspoon coarse sea salt
¼ teaspoon cracked black pepper
Olive oil–flavored cooking spray

1. Preheat oven to 375°.
2. Unroll dough onto an ungreased baking sheet, being careful not to separate into pieces. Gently press dough together along perforations to seal. Arrange lemon slices evenly over dough. Sprinkle evenly with rosemary leaves and next 3 ingredients; lightly coat with cooking spray. Place on bottom rack in oven, and bake at 375° for 14 minutes or until edges are golden. Cut into 8 equal portions. Serve warm. Yield: 8 servings.

Recipe Index

VEGETABLE COOKING CHART

Vegetable	Servings	Preparation	Cooking Instructions
Asparagus	3 to 4 per pound	Snap off tough ends. Remove scales, if desired.	To steam: Cook, covered, on a rack above boiling water 2 to 3 minutes. To boil: Cook, covered, in a small amount of boiling water 2 to 3 minutes or until crisp-tender.
Broccoli	3 to 4 per pound	Remove outer leaves and tough ends of lower stalks. Wash; cut into spears.	To steam: Cook, covered, on a rack above boiling water 5 to 7 minutes or until crisp-tender.
Carrots	4 per pound	Scrape; remove ends, and rinse. Leave tiny carrots whole; slice large carrots.	To steam: Cook, covered, on a rack above boiling water 8 to 10 minutes or until crisp-tender. To boil: Cook, covered, in a small amount of boiling water 8 to 10 minutes or until crisp-tender.
Cauliflower	4 per medium head	Remove outer leaves and stalk. Wash. Break into florets.	To steam: Cook, covered, on a rack above boiling water 5 to 7 minutes or until crisp-tender.
Corn	4 per 4 large ears	Remove husks and silks. Leave corn on the cob, or cut off kernels.	Cook, covered, in boiling water to cover 8 to 10 minutes (on cob) or in a small amount of boiling water 4 to 6 minutes (kernels).
Green beans	4 per pound	Wash; trim ends, and remove strings. Cut into 1½-inch pieces.	To steam: Cook, covered, on a rack above boiling water 5 to 7 minutes. To boil: Cook, covered, in a small amount of boiling water 5 to 7 minutes or until crisp-tender.
Potatoes	3 to 4 per pound	Scrub; peel, if desired. Leave whole, slice, or cut into chunks.	To boil: Cook, covered, in boiling water to cover 30 to 40 minutes (whole) or 15 to 20 minutes (slices or chunks). To bake: Bake at 400° for 1 hour or until done.
Snow peas	4 per pound	Wash; trim ends, and remove tough strings.	To steam: Cook, covered, on a rack above boiling water 2 to 3 minutes. Or sauté in cooking spray or 1 teaspoon oil over medium-high heat 3 to 4 minutes or until crisp-tender.
Squash, summer	3 to 4 per pound	Wash; trim ends, and slice or chop.	To steam: Cook, covered, on a rack above boiling water 6 to 8 minutes. To boil: Cook, covered, in a small amount of boiling water 6 to 8 minutes or until crisp-tender.
Squash, winter (including acorn, butternut, and buttercup)	2 per pound	Rinse; cut in half, and remove all seeds. Leave in halves to bake, or peel and cube to boil.	To boil: Cook cubes, covered, in boiling water 20 to 25 minutes. To bake: Place halves, cut sides down, in a shallow baking dish; add ½ inch water. Bake, uncovered, at 375° for 30 minutes. Turn and season, or fill; bake an additional 20 to 30 minutes or until tender.